THE BEST OF EPICURE'S

Entertaining With Asha Khatau

Popular Prakashan
www.popularprakashan.com

Published by
Harsha Bhatkal for
POPULAR PRAKASHAN PVT. LTD.
301, Mahalaxmi Chambers
22, Bhulabhai Desai Road
Mumbai – 400 026
www.popularprakashan.com

First Published 2013

(4368)
ISBN: 978-81-7991-809-8

Design: Mahendra Ghanekar, Anjali Sawant
Photography: Sumeet Ballal

Printed in India
by Thomson Press (India) Ltd.

Dedication

I dedicate this book to my close friends Madhu and Ravi Ruia who really love to entertain and they do it with style and elegance!

Acknowledgements

I sincerely thank the one above for giving me the ability and the capacity to write yet another book to my Epicure Series. I want to thank my mother-in-law Leela Khatau for giving me constant encouragement and support in all I do. I remember my late mother Sudha Sampat for long-lasting encouragement and courage that she gave me all my life. I sincerely thank my husband Mahendra Khatau for his constructive suggestions and moral support in whatever I do. Help from my three children, Priya, Shreya and Manish is always there; I thank them from my heart. My special thanks to Abhaji Singhania, Madhu Ruia and Niti Desai for all the help extended during the photo shoot. I appreciate and thank my dedicated staff Gopinath, Mahadev, Naresh, Dattu and Vijay who are always willing to work and help. I thank everyone on the team of my publisher Popular Prakashan, who is associated with this book, for their help and co-operation.

Contents

MULTI-CUISINE

Author's Note

Entertaining involves a lot of talent. Planning, selecting good décor, preparing the guest list, worrying about the table setting, the bar setting; planning the menu meticulously, making sure that each and every course is cooked to perfection, deciding the serving style, are just a few of the things, to name a few. Entertaining is an art. And the art of entertaining is the fine art of doing everything to perfection, yet not overdoing it. Cooking—itself an art—is about interpreting a recipe and producing unique results.

The most difficult part after menu-planning is shopping of ingredients and storing them until ready to use. Making the list, checking it out and then heading out to the market is the right way to operate. You need to do all of this well in time, too. The most important part of having a party is the menu. Careful planning and plenty of preparation before hand will ensure perfection. Make full use of what is available, using the freshest vegetables and seasonal fruits.

Do include different flavours and textures in the dishes. It is essential to include some cold dishes to make a meal 'flow'. There should be one item on the table that is fairly large and attractive-looking; perhaps a salad or main course which is the backbone of a menu. Dessert should be made with extra care and will add to the lasting impressions. Preparation for serving of coffee, tea, liquors etc. can be arranged on a side board. Always provide extra quantity of ingredients so one doesn't run around last minute.

Usually the table should be laid a day ahead, along with crockery, cutlery, linen, glassware and name labels placed in respective serving dishes. Flowers add a lot of elegance. Lighting plays an important role. It should be low enough to lend an intimate atmosphere, yet bright enough for guest to see easily. Candles are delightful and spread soft gentle light around.

I believe that the person who cooks must be the star of each and every recipe. Success lies in being confident and ready with advance preparation. No cook/host/hostess should be too busy to miss out on the fun of the occasion–and so often majority of the recipes can be prepared a few hours or may be a couple of days ahead. This basic prior organisation takes the strain out of the evening for the host and hostess.

Just before the expected time of arrival of your guests, make certain the table is laid, the flowers are sprayed with water, the lighting is as one would want it, background music is ready to be played, the temperature of the room is right, white wine and beer are in the fridge, red wine bottle opened and transferred into decanter, soft drinks and ice cubes ordered and chilled, the cold appetizers are placed on coffee tables and bar counter. Have a quick look at the cloak room to ensure all amenities are there. Nothing need be lavish, or beyond the capabilities of your purse. However, the right combination, carefully directed can be especially effective.

Here I present a collection of recipes that will fit into different themes and can be used as per your taste, inclination or occasion for those who hone the art of entertaining at home. Cooking is a joy, a therapy and happiness! Hope all you readers find this volume useful.

I wish luck and happiness with your cooking!

Glamourous Ladies Luncheon

Rosè Wine Punch

Serves 6

INGREDIENTS

½ cup melon wedges
½ cup peach wedges
½ cup seedless segments of tangerine
1 bottle Rosè wine
500 ml Sprite or Lemonade
Ice cubes, as required

To garnish
Additional fruit slices

METHOD

Place all the sliced fruit in a large pitcher and pour three cups of rosè wine over. Cover and set aside for 1 hour at room temperature. Strain the mixture, pressing lightly to extract fruit pulp into a punch bowl. Add fresh fruit slices, Sprite or Lemonade and the remaining wine. Divide equally into six pilsner glasses. Add ice and serve immediately.

(Image on page 27)

Gazpacho Shots

Makes 20 shot glasses

INGREDIENTS

1 kg tomatoes
1 stock cube
1 small onion, chopped
3 tbsp olive oil
¼ cup red wine vinegar
¼ cup cucumber, chopped
¼ cup red pepper, chopped
¼ cup fresh coriander, chopped
Salt to taste
Pepper to taste
Lemon juice to taste
Tabasco sauce to taste
Worcestershire sauce to taste

For topping
½ cup finely chopped cucumber
½ cup finely chopped green pepper
2 stalks celery, finely chopped
2-3 tbsp fresh chives, finely chopped
Salt to taste
Pepper to taste
20 pieces melba toast

To serve
Bread sticks

METHOD

Blanch the tomatoes and pass through a sieve to get the juice. Boil the tomato juice with the stock cube and cool. Purée the onion along with the olive oil and wine vinegar in a blender; add the tomato juice, cucumber, pepper, coriander and blend to mix well. You could use additional tomato juice to thin it if you wish.

Season well with salt, pepper and lemon juice. Add Tabasco and Worcestershire sauce to taste. Transfer the mixture to a large bowl and refrigerate to chill for 1-6 hours. Mix all the ingredients for topping except the toast, in a bowl and refrigerate to chill.

To serve, pour the soup in shot glasses, spoon the topping on each melba toast and place the toast resting on the rim of the glass. Arrange all these glasses over ice in a large tray.

Sun-dried Tomato Spread

Makes 2 cups

INGREDIENTS

100 gm sun-dried tomatoes
1 tbsp chopped garlic
¼ cup chopped almonds or pine nuts
3 tbsp chopped onion
¼ cup Balsamic vinegar
⅓ cup crushed tomatoes
¼ cup red wine vinegar
2 tbsp chopped fresh basil
2 tbsp chopped fresh parsley
½ cup olive oil
½ cup grated Parmesan cheese
Salt to taste
Pepper to taste

To garnish

Fresh basil leaves

To serve

Salted crackers or melba toast

METHOD

Place sun-dried tomatoes in a bowl and cover with hot water for 5 minutes, or until tender. In a food processor or blender, combine the sun-dried tomatoes, garlic, pine nuts and onion; process until well blended.

Add vinegar, crushed tomatoes and red wine vinegar, and process to a coarse paste. Transfer to a bowl and fold in basil, parsley, olive oil and Parmesan cheese. Add salt and pepper to taste. Garnish with fresh basil leaves and serve with crackers or melba toast.

(Image on page 27)

Labneh

Lebanese Cream Cheese

Makes 2 cups

INGREDIENTS

8 cups yogurt
1 tsp salt
2-3 tbsp olive oil + to drizzle

To garnish
Zatar spice mix

To serve
Pita bread

METHOD

Line a large sieve with cheesecloth and set the sieve over a bowl to collect the stock. Add the salt to the yogurt; mix well and pour into the cheesecloth. Place it in the refrigerator for 24 hours. Transfer the cheese to a bowl; add olive oil and mix well.

Smoothen the surface and make a pattern with a fork, drizzle olive oil, garnish with zatar spice mix and serve with pita bread.

(Image on page 27)

Pesto Hummus

Makes 1 cup

INGREDIENTS

100 gm chickpeas, soaked and boiled
2 tbsp tahina paste
2 tbsp olive oil
2 tbsp lemon juice
Salt to taste
2 tbsp pesto sauce

To garnish
Olive oil and sliced black olives

To serve
Crisp pita bread triangles

METHOD

Place all the ingredients except pesto in a blender jar and blend until smooth. If the mixture is too dry, add a little water.

Transfer to a serving bowl, drop pesto in the centre and swirl it into hummus to give double-coloured effect. Garnish with olive oil and black olives. Serve with crisp pita bread.

Mien Cum

Thai-style Lettuce Wrap

Serves 6-8

INGREDIENTS

1 tbsp sesame oil
2 tbsp finely chopped ginger
2 tbsp finely chopped garlic
2 tbsp finely chopped red chillies
2 tbsp finely chopped lemon grass
½ cup chopped onion
½ cup toasted coconut flakes
½ cup roasted and crushed peanuts
½ cup grated unripe green mango
½ cup chopped mushrooms
¼ cup finely chopped pepper
¼ cup finely chopped spring onion
2 tbsp finely chopped fresh coriander
1 large head iceberg lettuce
1 cup boiled and fried rice noodles

For sauce

¼ cup powdered peanuts
2 tbsp brown sugar
1 tbsp vinegar
1 tsp soy sauce
1 tsp chilli sauce
Salt to taste

METHOD

For the sauce, mix all the ingredients together with one-fourth cup water in a pan and heat till sugar is dissolved and mixture is thick. Pour in a serving bowl and set aside.

Heat oil in a frying pan; fry ginger, garlic, red chillies, lemon grass and onion until soft. Add the remaining ingredients except lettuce and noodles and cook briskly. Keep the mixture warm on a sizzler plate.

To serve, fold a lettuce leaf into a cone. Place a spoonful of mixture in the cup, a teaspoon of the sauce and sprinkle crushed fried noodles.

Note: Each person may assemble his or her own cup.

Quinoa Sushi Rolls

Serves 6-8

INGREDIENTS

4 (8-inch x 7-inch) nori sheets

1 cup uncooked quinoa (brown or white)

2 tbsp rice vinegar

2 tbsp black and white sesame seeds

½ tsp salt

2 tbsp sugar

For sushi roll filling

1 medium cucumber, peeled, thinly sliced and salted

2 tbsp sliced and pickled ginger

Thin strips of fried tofu

Thin strips of avocado

3 tbsp pickled radish

To serve

Kikkoman soy sauce, wasabi paste, pickled ginger and togarashi

METHOD

Cook quinoa in two cups of boiling water until all the water is absorbed. Cover and set aside for 10 minutes. In a small pan, mix vinegar, sesame seeds, salt and sugar over low heat. Cool to room temperature over a bowl of ice water.

Toss quinoa over a chopping board with vinegar dressing; do not add all the dressing or quinoa will get mushy. Add as much as it can absorb. Use wooden spoon to toss. Cover with damp cloth and set aside. Prepare the filling as mentioned above.

Toast a nori sheet on a burner and make it slightly wet with water. Place it on a bamboo mat. Spread two to three tablespoons of quinoa mixture on three-fourth of the nori, leaving one to two inches at the margins.

At the edge of the sheet over the quinoa, place any of the filling ingredients. Lift the mat and roll once to make sushi log. Slightly squeeze along entire roll. Lift the mat and roll again till you get to the end of the sheet.

The roll should be tight with filling in the centre. Cling wrap each roll and chill in the refrigerator for 30-40 minutes. Remove and cut with sharp knife into one-and-a-half-inch rolls. Place them on a flat plate and serve with soy sauce, wasabi paste, pickled ginger and togarashi.

(Image on page 27)

Garden Salad Appetiser Bowl

Serves 4-6

INGREDIENTS

For salad

4 tbsp Vinaigrette Dressing (page 202)

2 tbsp finely chopped mint

500 gm baby potatoes, boiled in salted water

225 gm broccoli florets

100 gm baby corn or snow peas

2 medium carrots

4 thick celery sticks

1 medium yellow pepper

1 medium red pepper

1 small head Romaine or any other lettuce

For mustard dip

½ cup soured cream

3 tbsp thick mayonnaise

2 tsp balsamic vinegar

1½ tsp grainy mustard

Brown sugar to taste

Salt to taste

Pepper to taste

METHOD

Combine vinaigrette and mint in a medium bowl and toss hot potatoes until well coated. Set aside to cool, stirring occasionally. Cut broccoli into bite-sized florets. Blanch the broccoli florets, baby corn or snow peas for 2 minutes in boiling water.

Drain and toss immediately in cold water and drain thoroughly when cold. Cut carrots, celery and peppers into 3-inch long sticks and plunge them in cold water. Drain and set aside. Separate leaves of lettuce and drop them in cold water and drain.

Arrange the vegetables attractively in a fairly shallow bowl with the potatoes piled up in the centre. Cover with cling film until ready to serve.

For mustard dip, combine the soured cream, mayonnaise, vinegar, mustard, sugar, salt and pepper. Mix well until well combined. Cover and chill. Serve the dip separately with chilled vegetables.

Salad Sticks

Serves 4-6

INGREDIENTS

1 red pepper
1 yellow pepper
1 green pepper
8 button mushrooms
8 ears of baby corn
A few lettuce leaves
100 gm mozzarella or Cheddar cheese
8 cherry tomatoes

For marinade

¼ cup olive oil
2 tbsp cider vinegar
2 tbsp finely chopped basil
1 tsp garlic salt
1 tsp pepper
1 tsp mustard powder

To serve

Barbeque sticks or toothpicks

METHOD

Cut peppers, mushrooms, baby corn, lettuce and cheese into even-sized cubes. Cut cherry tomatoes in halves. Thread all the ingredients onto barbeque sticks or toothpicks in the following order: one cube each of red, yellow and green peppers, mushroom, baby corn, cherry tomato, lettuce and cheese. Arrange all the sticks on a serving plate and set aside.

Mix all the ingredients for the marinade in a small bowl. Drizzle the marinade all over the salad sticks. Cover with cling film and chill in the refrigerator until ready to serve.

Spicy Fried Nuts

Makes ½ cup

INGREDIENTS

1 tsp oil + for deep-frying
½ cup peanuts or cashew nuts
1 spring onion stalk, chopped
2-3 fresh red chillies, cut into thick slices
½ tsp salt

To garnish

Crisp fried basil leaves

METHOD

Heat sufficient oil and deep-fry the nuts until golden. Drain on absorbent paper. Heat one teaspoon oil in a frying pan; toss spring onion and chillies for one minute. Add the nuts and salt. Toss again. Remove from heat and set aside to cool. Garnish with fried basil leaves and serve.

Chilled Lettuce Soup

Serves 6

INGREDIENTS

1 cup finely chopped onions, scallions, and/or shallots

1 clove garlic, chopped

3 tbsp butter

¾ tsp coriander powder

¾ tsp salt + to taste

¼ tsp black pepper + to taste

¾ cup diced potato

8 cups (350 gm) coarsely chopped lettuce leaves

1 cup White Vegetable Stock (recipe follows)

To garnish

Thick cream

METHOD

Sauté onion and garlic in 2 tablespoons butter for 1 minute. Add 3 cups water and cook over moderately low heat, stirring, until softened, or for 3-5 minutes.

Add coriander powder, ¾ teaspoon salt, and ¼ teaspoon pepper and cook for 1 minute. Stir in potato, lettuce, and the stock, bring to a boil, reduce heat and simmer, covered, until potato is tender, about 10 minutes.

Purée soup in batches in a blender (use caution when blending hot liquids) and transfer to a pan. Bring soup to a simmer, stir in remaining butter and salt and pepper to taste. Chill the soup for several hours. Serve in small glasses, garnished with a swirl of cream.

White Vegetable Stock

Heat 2 tbsp oil in a large pan over moderate heat and add 4 chopped carrots, 4 chopped celery stalks, 100 gm chopped bottle gourd, 1 large chopped leek, 2-3 chopped onions, 2 chopped sprigs of parsley, 2 black peppercorns, 2 bay leaves, 2 chopped garlic cloves, 2 tbsp salt, and 2 vegetable stock cubes (optional), along with 6 cups water and stir once it comes to a boil. Simmer for 30 minutes. Discard the bay leaf and process in a blender and strain into a bowl and set aside until ready to use.

Baked Tofu and Green Beans Salad with Tahini Dressing

Serves 6-8

INGREDIENTS

400 gm firm tofu

For marinade

5 tbsp lemon juice

1 tbsp balsamic vinegar

1 tbsp soy sauce

1 tbsp olive oil

1 tsp freshly ground pepper

1 tsp lemon rind

For salad

2 cups green beans, trimmed and cut into 1-inch pieces

2-3 stalks finely chopped spring onions

2 tbsp finely chopped parsley

For tahina dressing

¼ cup tahina paste

1 tbsp soy sauce

1 tbsp rice vinegar

1 tbsp sesame oil

1 large clove garlic

2 tbsp diced green pepper

2 tbsp lemon juice

1 tsp sugar

To garnish

A few salad greens

1 cup cherry tomatoes, grapes and/or gooseberries

¼ cup toasted black and white sesame seeds

To serve

Crisp lavash

METHOD

Cut tofu in 2-inch by ½-inch pieces. Mix all the ingredients for the marinade in a small bowl and brush tofu pieces with the marinade. Marinate for 30 to 40 minutes. Bake the tofu in an oven at 180°C/350°F/Gas Mark 4 for 20 to 25 minutes, turning once in between. Remove from oven and set aside.

For the salad, steam the green beans until tender and rinse with cold water. Set aside. For tahina dressing, blend all the ingredients in a small blender jar until mixed well.

To assemble the salad, mix together the beans, spring onions and parsley in a bowl and toss with enough of tahina dressing to coat the vegetables. Line a round platter with crisp salad greens.

Arrange the beans and tofu pieces over it in circular pattern towards the rim. Mound cherry tomatoes, grapes and gooseberries in the centre of the plate in a circle. Drizzle remaining tahina dressing all over.

Finally sprinkle with toasted sesame seeds. Arrange lavash pieces in a decorative manner (e.g. place them standing all around the rim etc.). Serve cold.

Tips: 1) Soak store-bought tofu in chilled mineral water before use.
2) Tear salad greens instead of chopping them and soak in ice cold water and rinse before use.

Beans, Nuts and Vegetables Trio Salad

Serves 6

INGREDIENTS

For salad

½ cup red kidney beans

½ cup white cannelline beans

½ cup fresh soy beans (edamame), boiled (optional)

2 tbsp virgin olive oil

150 gm French beans, cut into 1-inch pieces and blanched

1 small red or yellow pepper, thinly sliced

1 medium carrot, coarsely grated

2 tbsp chopped sun-dried tomatoes

2 tbsp shallots

¼ cup split almonds

¼ cup cashew nuts

For dressing

3 tbsp grape seed or walnut oil

2 tbsp red wine vinegar

1 tbsp Dijon mustard

1 tsp sugar

1 tsp dried mixed herbs

Salt to taste

Pepper to taste

To garnish

Fresh herbs, shredded Romaine lettuce and halved cherry tomatoes

METHOD

Soak both the beans overnight and boil in open pan separately. Make sure beans are *al dente* (cooked yet firm to the bite). Drain and toss beans with olive oil. Set aside for 30 minutes. In another large bowl, mix together prepared vegetables, sun-dried tomatoes, shallots and tossed beans.

For the dressing, place all the ingredients in a screw top jar and shake well.

Toss the salad with the dressing and adjust the seasoning. Sprinkle nuts on top and toss gently. Transfer the salad on a serving platter laced with shredded lettuce. Arrange the halved cherry tomatoes, closer to the rim of the plate. Garnish with herbs and serve at room temperature.

Salade Provençale

Serves 8

INGREDIENTS

For salad

8 cups salad greens, torn into square pieces, washed and chilled

½ cup sliced black olives

4-5 small white onions, thinly sliced and soaked in water with sugar

2 medium ripe tomatoes, cut into wedges

½ cup toasted herbed croûtons

½ cup mixed seeds (sunflower, pumpkin etc.) and cranberries

For dressing

½ cup Mayonnaise (page 202)

⅓ cup cider or wine vinegar

2 tbsp corn syrup or (1 tsp cornflour + 2 tbsp water, heated)

2 tbsp olive oil

1 tbsp lemon juice

1 tbsp sugar

1 large clove garlic, crushed

½ tsp Italian seasoning

½ tsp dried parsley

Salt to taste

To garnish

Freshly grated Parmesan cheese, freshly ground black pepper

To serve

Crusty bread

METHOD

For the dressing, mix all the ingredients in a blender jar and blend until smooth. Set aside.

Prepare all the vegetables for the salad as per instruction given and chill. Divide all the salad ingredients in two parts. Take a large transparent glass bowl; layer half of each ingredient in given order. Drizzle one-third of prepared dressing over the salad and toss gently to mix.

Top the salad with remaining ingredients in the same fashion, reserving some croûtons for garnishing and tossing with another one-third of the dressing. Serve garnished with grated Parmesan cheese and pepper powder with crusty bread and extra dressing at the side.

Red Pepper Mousse

Serves 4-6

INGREDIENTS

1 tbsp olive oil

1 tbsp chopped garlic

500 gm red peppers, roasted and peeled

1 tbsp grenadine syrup

1 tbsp lemon juice

2 tbsp Mayonnaise (page 202)

½ cup grated cheese

Salt to taste

Pepper to taste

1 tbsp gelatine, dissolved in
¼ cup Vegetable Stock (recipe follows)

½ cup fresh cream

To garnish

A sprig of parsley and toasted pine nuts

To serve

Crisp bread or crackers

METHOD

Heat oil in a frying pan and fry garlic and peppers for 2 to 3 minutes. Remove from heat and set aside to cool. Place sautéed peppers and garlic in a blender jar and add grenadine syrup, lemon juice, mayonnaise, grated cheese, salt and pepper. Blend until smooth.

While the motor is running, add gelatine mixture in a thin stream. Mix well. Transfer the mixture into a bowl.

Beat the cream to form soft peaks and fold the cream into the pepper mixture. Transfer this to a serving bowl and refrigerate until set. Remove and garnish with parsley and pine nuts. Serve with crisp bread or crackers.

Vegetable Stock

Place 2 medium onions, chopped, 1 medium leek and carrot each, chopped, 1 large sprig parsley tied with 1 bay leaf, 1 small piece bottle gourd, chopped and 6 cups water in the pressure cookerand cook for 3 whistles. Cool and discard the bay leaf and parsley bunch, then blend, sieve and set aside.

Makes 4-5 cups

Roquette, Artichoke Heart and Almond Salad

Serves 4-6

INGREDIENTS

For salad

100 gm roquette leaves, cleaned and washed

½ cup halved cherry tomatoes

½ medium red pepper, thinly sliced

½ medium yellow pepper, thinly sliced

2 medium tomatoes, blanched and chopped

200 gm artichoke heart, cut into two

¼ cup slivered and toasted almonds

¼ cup grated Parmesan cheese

For dressing

3 tbsp olive oil

1 tbsp wine or balsamic vinegar

1 tbsp Dijon mustard

1 tsp sugar

Salt to taste

Pepper to taste

METHOD

Prepare all the vegetables as mentioned above. Rinse each one in chilled water and drain completely. Pile up all the vegetables in a large bowl. Cover with cling wrap and chill until ready to serve. Mix all the ingredients for the dressing in a screw top jar. Shake vigorously to mix. Set aside.

At the time of serving, remove salad bowl from the refrigerator; pour dressing over and toss gently with salad spoon and fork in upward movement. Add almonds and Parmesan and toss again. Serve at once.

Peanut, Water Chestnut and Green Gram Salad

Serves 4-6

INGREDIENTS

200 gm water chestnuts, shelled and boiled

200 gm fresh green gram, shelled and boiled

100 gm raw peanuts, soaked for ½ hour and boiled

¼ cup soaked sago

Juice of half a lemon

Salt to taste

Pepper to taste

Cumin powder to taste

Garnish

Finely chopped fresh coriander

To serve

Shredded carrots, beetroot and green papaya, as required

METHOD

Mix together water chestnut, green gram and peanuts in a bowl. Add the remaining ingredients and toss to mix. Cover and chill. Garnish with chopped coriander and serve on bed of shredded vegetables.

Thai Crunch Salad

Serves 4-6

INGREDIENTS

1 head (250 gm) Chinese cabbage, cut into ¼-inch strips

1 small (200 gm) red cabbage, cored and chopped long

2 large carrots, peeled and cut into strips

1 large cucumber, peeled, cored and cut into strips

2 large tomatoes, cored and chopped

2 medium avocados, chopped (optional)

2 bunches spring onions, thinly sliced

1 bunch (approx. 1½ cups) coriander leaves, finely chopped

2 cups cooked green soy beans (edamame)

2 cups roasted and coarsely chopped peanuts

4 cups fried wonton chips

1 recipe Lime-Coriander Dressing (recipe follows)

2 cups boiled and fried rice sticks

1 recipe Thai Peanut Dressing (recipe follows)

To garnish

Celery leaves, toasted peanuts, halved cherry tomatoes and lemon slices

To serve

Banana leaf lined plate

METHOD

Place both the cabbages, carrots, cucumber, tomatoes, avocados, spring onion, coriander leaves, soy beans and peanuts in a large mixing bowl and toss to mix. Set aside. Just before serving, place wonton chips in a small bowl and toss with lime-coriander dressing. Place prepared vegetables on a banana leaf lined plate. Top with tossed wonton chips. Sprinkle rice sticks over the salad. Fill peanut dressing in a squeeze bottle or syrup dispenser and drizzle over rice sticks. Garnish with celery leaves, peanuts, cherry tomato and lemon slices. Serve immediately.

Lime-Coriander Dressing

Blend together ¼ small red pepper cored and cubed, ½ cup chopped coriander leaves, 1½ tbsp honey, 1½ tbsp rice vinegar, 2 tbsp lemon juice, 2 tsp Dijon mustard, ½ tsp sesame oil, ½ tsp minced ginger, salt to taste, pepper to taste, ⅓-½ cup extra virgin olive oil, in a small blender jar, process until smooth. Transfer to a bowl and set aside.

Makes approx. 1 cup

Thai Peanut Dressing

Blend together 2 tbsp peanut butter, 1 tbsp sugar, 1 tbsp rice vinegar, 1 tbsp soy sauce, 1 tbsp lemon juice, 1½ tsp sesame oil, ¾ tsp salt, ¼ tsp black pepper, ¼ tsp chilli flakes in a blender jar with 2 tablespoons water until smooth. Use immediately or refrigerate until ready to use. Use at room temperature.

Makes ½ cup

(Image on page 28)

Rosè Wine Punch
Sun-dried Tomato Spread
Labneh
Grape and Melon Delight
Quinoa Sushi Rolls

Thai Crunch Salad
Stone-grilled Vegetables with Aglio-Olio Pasta and Arrabbiata Sauce
Ginger and Orange Cupcakes

Stone-grilled Vegetables with Aglio-Olio Pasta and Arrabbiata Sauce

Serves 8

INGREDIENTS

For vegetables

500 gm mixed vegetables of your choice (brinjals, onions, peppers, asparagus, zucchini, broccoli etc.)

2 tbsp olive oil

1 tbsp freshly chopped herbs

1 tbsp chopped garlic

1 tbsp balsamic vinegar

Salt to taste

Pepper to taste

Chilli flakes to taste

For pasta

200 gm packaged pasta of your choice

3 tbsp olive oil

6 cloves garlic, crushed

1 tbsp basil, chopped

Chilli flakes to taste

Salt to taste

Black pepper to taste

For arrabbiata sauce

2 tbsp olive oil

2 medium onions, finely chopped

2 cloves garlic, crushed

200 gm tomatoes, blanched and coarsely chopped

2 tbsp tomato purée

1 tsp sugar

1 tsp salt

1 tsp freshly ground pepper

1 tbsp chilli flakes

2 tbsp fresh cream

1 tsp dried oregano

To garnish

Grated Parmesan cheese and freshly chopped herbs

To serve

Toasted garlic bread

METHOD

For grilled vegetables, heat a 12 or 14-inch round stone in the oven for 8-10 minutes. Cut all the vegetables into 2-inch sticks and place them on the heated stone. Drizzle olive oil; toss gently until it coats the vegetables. Sprinkle herbs, garlic, balsamic vinegar, salt, pepper and chilli flakes, toss again. Place under the grill for 7-8 minutes. Remove and set aside.

For pasta, boil the pasta in salted water, until soft but firm, approx. 6-7 minutes. Drain and place under running cold water. Drain all the water out. In a large frying pan, heat olive oil, add garlic, basil and chilli flakes. Cook for 1-2 minutes. Add drained pasta, salt and pepper; toss gently and set aside.

For arrabbiata sauce, in a pan, heat oil, add onions and garlic, cook over medium heat until soft. Add tomatoes, tomato purée, sugar, salt, pepper and chilli flakes. Simmer for 30 minutes, stirring occasionally. Remove and set aside to cool. Blend ½ the sauce in a processor to smooth paste. Mix it with remaining sauce, adjust seasoning. Add the cream and oregano. Serve warm with pasta. Makes 1½ cups.

To assemble, reheat and place pasta on a serving dish. Cover with prepared arrabbiata sauce to form 2-inch thick border on outer side. Place hot grilled vegetables in the centre of the dish. Garnish with Parmesan cheese and herbs. Serve hot with garlic bread.

(Image on page 28)

Chiang Mai Curry Noodles

Serves 6

Kao Soi

INGREDIENTS

2 tbsp vegetable oil
1 tbsp finely chopped garlic
2 tsp curry powder
2 tbsp red curry paste
200 gm mixed vegetables, cut into strips
1¾ cup Vegetable Stock (page 23)
200 gm tofu
2 cups coconut milk
2 tbsp lemon juice
2 tbsp soy sauce
Salt to taste
Sugar to taste
400 gm thin rice noodles, blanched and kept warm
⅓ cup shallots
⅓ cup spring onions
⅓ cup freshly chopped coriander

To garnish

Thin stalks of spring onions, fresh red chillies and lemon wedges

METHOD

Heat oil in a thick-bottomed pan; fry garlic, curry powder and red curry paste for 1 minute. Add vegetables and vegetable stock. Mix well. Cook for 2-3 minutes. Add tofu and coconut milk; simmer for 4-5 minutes. Add lemon juice, soy sauce, salt and sugar to taste. At the time of serving, take individual soup bowl, place handful of noodles and divide the shallots, spring onion and coriander equally among the bowls. Ladle prepared curry sauce over it to ¾-bowl full. Garnish with spring onion, red chillies and lemon wedges. Serve right away.

Creole-Style Baked Vegetables

Serves 8

INGREDIENTS

500 gm brinjal, sliced diagonally
1 tablespoon oil + for greasing
1 celery stalk, sliced diagonally
2 medium red peppers, cut in strips
150 gm lima or kidney beans, soaked and boiled
250 gm corn kernels, boiled
½ cup breadcrumbs
½ cup grated cheese
1 medium onion, chopped
4 large tomatoes, sliced
1 tsp chopped fresh basil
1 tsp oregano
2 jalapeño chillies, thinly sliced
Salt to taste
Pepper to taste
Butter to grease

METHOD

Toss brinjal with one tablespoon oil and steam until soft. Remove and set aside. Blanch celery in boiling salted water. Add peppers and lima beans, and cook until just tender; during last thirty seconds, add corn (do not overcook), and drain the cooked vegetables.

Grease a large baking dish with oil, and sprinkle with half of breadcrumbs and cheese; add a layer of corn-bean mixture and three-fourth of the brinjals. Combine onion, tomatoes and basil; spoon a layer of onion-tomato mixture over the brinjal layer. Sprinkle with chillies, season with salt and pepper.

Dot with butter, and sprinkle with breadcrumbs again. Repeat layering until casserole is filled. Toss remaining brinjal with remaining breadcrumbs and lightly sauté in oil. Top the dish with tossed brinjal and remaining cheese. Lightly bake uncovered at 150°C/300°F/Gas Mark 2 for 45 minutes. Serve hot.

Tofu Cheesecake

Serves 6-8

INGREDIENTS

Base

200 gm digestive biscuit
50 gm melted butter
¼ cup powdered sugar

Cheesecake

5 gm China grass mixed with 5 tbsp water or 4 tsp gelatine mixed with ¼ cup liquid

200 gm soft silken tofu
200 gm condensed milk
100 gm fresh cream
Preferred Flavourings (recipes follow)
1 tbsp lemon juice

Garnish

Whipped cream and relevant topping

METHOD

For the base, process the biscuits in a blender to crumble them, or alternatively you could break the biscuits up on a greaseproof paper by covering the paper with another piece and firmly roll a rolling pin to and fro until the biscuits become crumbs. Melt butter in a pan and add biscuit crumbs and sugar.

Mix well. Remove from heat and line the base and sides of a 9-inch or 10-inch loose bottom cake tin with the biscuit crumbs and press it with the back of your hand to spread evenly. Bake it in hot oven at 180°C/350°F/Gas Mark 4 for 5-7 minutes and set aside to cool.

For the cheesecake, mix china grass or gelatine with water or preferred liquid and heat gently, stirring continuously. Remove from heat and set aside to cool. Strain the gelatine mixture through a fine sieve.

Process tofu and condensed milk in a blender jar and empty in a large bowl. Beat the cream until thick and add to the tofu mixture and gently fold in the preferred flavouring spoon by spoon, in upward movement, along with lemon juice.

Add cooled gelatine mixture in a thin stream making sure each addition is incorporated. Mix well. Pour this mixture over the prepared and lined tin. Cover and chill in the refrigerator for 2-4 hours. Remove from the tin onto a serving plate and garnish with whipped cream and flavouring ingredient of your choice.

Preferred Flavouring Suggestions:

Mango Cheesecake: Peel and take out pulp of 2 ripe Alphonso mangoes and add to the basic mixture. Slice 1 mango into thin wedges and reserve for decoration along with whipped cream.

Lemon Cheesecake: Fold in the juice of 2 lemons and grated rind of 1 lemon into the basic mixture.

Kiwi Cheesecake: Process chopped 2-3 kiwi fruit with 1 tbsp kiwi liqueur and 1 tbsp icing sugar. Line a cooled spring form tin base with extra slices of kiwi and fill half the cheese mixture. As it sets, spread further kiwi slices on the top and then cover with remaining cheesecake mixture. Decorate with sweetened cream and kiwi slices or an orchid flower in the centre.

Strawberry Cheesecake: Process 250 gm fresh strawberries with 1 tbsp brandy and 1 tbsp icing sugar. Proceed the same way as the kiwi recipe.

Blueberry Cheesecake: ½ cup blueberry preserve mixed with 1 tsp lemon juice and little water or 250 gm fresh blueberries processed with 1 tsp lemon juice and a few blueberries (dried or fresh) to decorate.

Baked Fruit-Flavoured Yogurt

Serves 6

INGREDIENTS

2 cups thick yogurt

1 cup condensed milk

2 tbsp plain flour

For fruit topping

1 cup fruit juice of your choice

2-3 tbsp sugar

3 tbsp corn flour

1 tsp lemon juice

To garnish

Sprigs of mint and fruit slices

METHOD

Blend together yogurt, condensed milk and plain flour in a blender jar until smooth. Pour into 6 small ramekin dishes or 3 cup-sized shallow dish. Bake in a hot oven at 170°C/325°F/Gas Mark 3 for 30-40 minutes or until the top is golden. Remove and set aside to cool slightly.

Refrigerate until cold. For the fruit topping, mix all the ingredients together in a pan and cook on a medium heat, stirring all the time. Cook until thick and transparent. Spread over baked yogurt, garnish with sprigs of mint and fruit slices and serve.

Fruit Pie with Almond Crumb Topping

Serves 8

INGREDIENTS

1 (9-inch) ready baked pie crust or 20 tarts (recipe follows)

For crumb topping

½ cup blanched and sliced almonds

½ cup brown sugar

⅓ cup rolled oats

⅓ cup refined flour

Salt to taste

6 tbsp ice cold butter

For pie filling

1 tin (440 gm) cherry or strawberry or apple or peach topping

1 tsp lemon juice

¼ cup corn flour

To serve

Vanilla ice cream

METHOD

Bake a 9-inch pie crust or 20 small tarts of short crust pastry as per the recipe given below. Cool the crust to room temperature. Set aside. Preheat the oven to 180°C/350°F/ Gas Mark 4 while you make the topping.

For crumb topping, combine almonds, brown sugar, oats, flour, and salt in a large bowl. Work butter into the almond mixture with your fingers, breaking up any large pieces, until incorporated completely. Cover and chill for 15 minutes.

For pie filling, combine the topping of your choice, lemon juice and corn flour in a pan and cook gently. Stir until well combined. Cook for 3 to 4 minutes.

Pour this mixture onto the prepared pie crust or tart cases and smoothen the top surface. Crumble oat mixture (crumb topping) over the top.

Bake in the preheated oven for about 45 minutes or until the filling is bubbling and the crust and crumble topping are browned. Let cool completely. Cut the pie into wedges. Serve warm with vanilla ice cream.

Basic Short Crust Pastry

INGREDIENTS

200 gm sifted refined flour

½ tsp salt

2 tbsp powdered sugar (for sweet pastry)

100 gm cold butter, cut into cubes

METHOD

Preheat the oven to 180°C/350°F/Gas Mark 4 for 10-15 minutes. Place flour and salt in a shallow bowl. Rub butter in the flour using your finger tips. The mixture should resemble breadcrumbs. Make a well in the centre of the mixture. Add 2-3 tablespoons cold water, 1 tablespoon at a time and mix quickly to form a ball.

Cover with cling wrap and allow to rest for 30 minutes in the refrigerator. Remove from refrigerator and place the dough on a flat surface. Roll out the dough to 3 mm thickness. Lightly press rolled out dough into 9-inch round pie dish.

Prick the pastry lightly with a fork. Place the pastry in preheated oven on second rack from bottom. Bake blind for 12-15 minutes. Remove and set aside to cool.

Note: For small tarts use 12-14 individual tart cases. Roll out the dough and cut the pastry with 2-inch cutter. Gently press into 1½-inch tart case mould, prick with fork, arrange on a tray and bake for 10-12 minutes.

Grape and Melon Delight

Serves 4-6

INGREDIENTS

1 packet lemon jelly
1 tsp lemon juice
1 medium musk melon
100 gm grapes, red or green, chopped
½ cup whipping cream

METHOD

Make the jelly and allow it to cool. When it begins to thicken, add lemon juice. Cut the melon into basket shape. Leave a strip along the top, as a handle, and remove all the pulp leaving the shell intact. Chop the pulp into small cubes.

Mix the chopped melon and grapes with the jelly, reserving some for garnish. Whip the cream until soft peaks form and fold it in the fruit mixture.

Transfer the mixture into the melon basket and spread the reserved jelly over the top. Chill until set. Serve cold.

(Image on page 27)

Ginger and Orange Cupcakes

Makes 8-10 cupcakes

INGREDIENTS

1½ cups plain flour, sieved before measuring
¾ tsp baking powder
¾ tsp powdered cinnamon
¾ tsp soda bicarbonate
¾ tsp salt
1 tbsp grated ginger
1 tbsp chopped orange peel
⅓ cup salad oil
⅓ cup brown sugar
¼ cup condensed milk
⅓ cup powdered jaggery
Icing sugar, to sprinkle

METHOD

Sift together the plain flour, baking powder, powdered cinnamon, soda bicarbonate and salt. Place the mixture in a bowl. Make a well in the centre; add ginger, orange peel, oil, brown sugar and the condensed milk.

Mix jaggery in half cup of boiling water and add to the batter. Beat until smooth. Fill cup cake moulds up to three-fourth full and bake in a preheated oven at 180°C/350°F/Gas Mark 4 for 20 minutes or until golden.

Cool in the tin for 10 minutes and turn it out on a wire rack to cool. Sprinkle liberally with icing sugar.

Recommended frosting:

Cinnamon whipping cream or orange flavoured butter cream icing

(Image on page 28)

Executive Lunch

Lychee and Mint Mojito

Serves 2

INGREDIENTS

½ cup lychee juice
1 large lemon, cut into small pieces
10-12 fresh mint leaves
2 tbsp sugar syrup
¼ cup fresh pineapple juice
Ice, as required

To garnish
A few sprigs of mint

METHOD

Mix lychee juice, lemon pieces and mint leaves in cocktail shaker. Add sugar syrup, pineapple juice and ice and shake to blend well. Pour into tall glass, garnish with sprigs of mint and serve.

Pomegranate Caprioshka

Serves 1

INGREDIENTS

1 large lemon, cut into 8 pieces
6-8 fresh mint leaves
1-2 tbsp powdered sugar
2 tbsp fresh pomegranate kernels
¼ cup pomegranate juice
60 ml vodka (optional)
Crushed ice

To garnish
A dash of grenadine and wedge of lemon

METHOD

Place the lemon, mint leaves, sugar and pomegranate kernels in a stainless steel jug. Crush with a wooden pestle until partially crushed. Add the pomegranate juice and transfer the mixture to an old-fashioned glass. Add the vodka if using and fill up with crushed ice. Garnish with grenadine and a wedge of lemon.

Sesame-Crusted Tofu with Orange-Miso Sauce

Serves 8

INGREDIENTS

For tofu

400 gm silken tofu, cut into ½-inch cubes

2 tbsp sesame oil

Salt to taste

Pepper to taste

5 tbsp black and white sesame seeds, toasted

For orange-miso sauce

1 cup Mayonnaise (page 202)

2 tbsp orange juice

1 tbsp miso paste

1 tsp pure sesame oil

1 tsp grated fresh ginger

½ tsp grated orange rind

Salt to taste

Pepper to taste

To garnish

Sliced orange rind, as required

To serve

Cocktail toothpicks, as required

METHOD

For the orange-miso sauce, whisk all the ingredients together in a medium-sized bowl. Refrigerate until ready to use. Soak tofu pieces in chilled mineral water for 20-30 minutes. Drain and place them in a bowl and pour sesame oil over it. Toss gently to coat.

Sprinkle tofu pieces with salt and pepper. Place sesame seeds in a small plate. Coat each tofu piece with sesame seeds and arrange on greased baking tray. Bake in a preheated oven at 180°C/350°F/Gas Mark 4 for 5 minutes.

Transfer tofu pieces on a serving plate; garnish with orange rinds and serve warm with the bowl of orange-miso sauce and cocktail toothpicks at the side.

(Image on page 46)

Olive and Pepper Pinwheel Wrap

Makes 50 pieces

INGREDIENTS

1 cup (200 gm) cream cheese, softened
¾ cup (150 gm) feta cheese, crumbled
2 tbsp chopped black olives
2 tbsp chopped red pepper
1 cup Black Olive Tapenade (recipe follows)
1 cup shredded carrots
5 (6-inch) tortillas

To serve

Olive oil mixed with chilli flakes, to drizzle

METHOD

In a medium bowl, combine the cheeses, chopped olives and pepper. Mix well. Divide the mixture and spread evenly over each tortillas. Top the cream cheese layer with a thin layer of tapenade and sprinkle with shredded carrots. Tightly roll up each tortilla, pressing down gently to seal. Wrap each tortilla individually with a cling wrap and refrigerate for 3-4 hours. Slice each tortilla into 10 pinwheels. Drizzle little olive oil mixed with chilli flakes. Secure each piece with a toothpick and serve.

Black Olive Tapenade

Blend together 1 cup black olives, 1 tbsp each of capers, garlic, lemon juice, olive oil and 1 tsp dried herbs.

(Image on page 117)

Pan-Fried Dumplings

Serves 6

INGREDIENTS

12-15 wonton wrappers
200 gm tofu, crumbled
½ tsp sesame seeds
½ tsp corn flour
½ tsp salt
1 tsp sesame oil
1 tsp chopped green chillies
1 tsp garlic
2 tbsp finely chopped spring onions
4 tbsp sunflower oil or sesame oil

To serve

Korean Soy Sauce (recipe follows)

METHOD

In a small bowl, mix together tofu, sesame seeds, corn flour, salt, sesame oil, chillies, garlic and spring onions. Put 1 teaspoon of mixture in the centre of each wonton wrapper and fold it across to make a triangle and twist both the tips to make a hat shaped dumpling. Bring water to a boil in a large pan and drop 3-4 dumplings at a time. Cook for 3 minutes. Stir-fry the cooked dumplings in sunflower oil till golden. Remove and drain on absorbent paper. Serve hot with Korean soy sauce.

Korean Soy Sauce

In a serving bowl, mix together 3 tbsp soy sauce, 1 tbsp chopped spring onions, 1 tsp each of sesame seeds, oil, chopped red chilli, crushed garlic, sugar and vinegar.

Makes ⅓ cup

Tex-Mex Appetiser Tarts

Serves 10

INGREDIENTS

12-14 tart cases

For filling

½ cup grated Monetary Jack cheese

½ cup boiled corn

½ cup roasted and cubed red and yellow peppers

¼ cup Mayonnaise (page 202)

¼ cup chopped jalapeño chillies

¼ cup chopped fresh coriander

1 tsp oregano

1 tsp taco seasoning mix

1 tsp chilli flakes

For garnish

Sliced jalapeño, as required

To serve

Red Salsa (page 71), as required

Sour Cream (page 71), as required

METHOD

Mix all the ingredients for the filling in a bowl and mix well. Fill in the tart cases. Bake in the preheated oven at 180°C/350°F/Gas Mark 4 for 7-8 minutes or until the cheese has melted. Remove from the oven and allow it to cool slightly. Garnish with sliced jalapeños and serve with salsa and sour cream.

(Image on page 45)

Feta and Nut Spread

Serves 6-8

INGREDIENTS

225 gm crumbled feta cheese
2 tbsp olive oil
1 tbsp lemon juice
2 tbsp finely chopped pepper
2 tbsp pecan nuts or walnuts
1 tsp minced garlic
1 tsp chopped fresh oregano
½ tsp crushed red pepper
¼ tsp black pepper

To garnish

Chilli flakes, as required
Fresh herbs, as required
Chopped nuts, as required

To serve

Melba toast or salted crackers

METHOD

Process all the ingredients in food processor or mix thoroughly with a wooden spoon until well blended. Transfer into a serving bowl and chill for 2 hours in a refrigerator before serving. Place the bowl in the centre of a large platter, sprinkle with chilli flakes, fresh herbs and nuts. Serve with melba toast or salted crackers.

Hot and Sour Tofu Soup

Serves 6

INGREDIENTS

1 tbsp sesame oil
2 tbsp red Thai curry paste
6 cups water or thin stock
200 gm silken tofu, cut into cubes
200 gm mixed vegetables (baby corn, broccoli, spring onions, mushrooms, peppers, asparagus etc.)
2 tbsp tamarind purée
2 tsp freshly chopped turmeric
2 tsp brown sugar
1 tsp chopped red chillies
4-5 kaffir lime leaves
4-5 lemon grass stalks pieces
2 tbsp lemon juice
2 tbsp light soy sauce

To garnish

¼ cup chopped fresh coriander

METHOD

Heat oil in a pan, fry curry paste for 2 minutes. Add 3 cups of water or stock and tofu. Bring to a boil and simmer for 10 minutes. In another pan, boil remaining 3 cups of water or stock and add all the remaining ingredients and bring to a boil. Mix both the liquids into one pan and boil for another 2-3 minutes. Garnish with chopped coriander and serve.

(Image on page 46)

Cabbage and Carrot Soup

Serves 4-6

INGREDIENTS

1 large onion, chopped
2 cloves garlic, chopped
1 large carrot, chopped
1 celery stalk, chopped
1 tbsp olive oil
250 gm cabbage, chopped
250 gm ripe tomatoes, chopped
8 cups Vegetable Stock (page 23)
Salt to taste
Pepper to taste

METHOD

In a thick-bottomed pan, sauté onion, garlic, carrot and celery in oil for 5 minutes. Add remaining ingredients and bring to a boil. Reduce heat and simmer for 20-25 minutes. The cabbage should wilt. Remove from heat and cool. Blend and strain the soup. Return to heat and adjust the seasoning. Serve hot.

Moroccan Chickpea Salad

Serves 4

INGREDIENTS

For salad

1 cup chickpeas, soaked overnight, boiled and drained

1 medium red pepper, roasted, peeled and cubed

10-12 stuffed green olives, halved

2 tbsp capers

½ cup finely chopped fresh coriander

For dressing

1 levelled tsp cumin-coriander powder

1 levelled tsp cinnamon powder

½ tsp chilli flakes

2 tbsp olive oil

1 tbsp cider vinegar or lemon juice

½ tsp oregano

½ tsp sugar

½ tsp mustard

Salt to taste

Pepper to taste

To garnish

Toasted pine nuts, as required

10-12 mint leaves, roughly chopped

METHOD

Place drained chickpeas in a bowl; slightly crush the chickpeas with a fork so that they can absorb the flavours better. Add the pepper, olives, capers and three-fourth of the chopped coriander. Toss gently to mix. Combine all the ingredients for the dressing in a bowl and add to the prepared salad. Mix well. Garnish with pine nuts, chopped mint leaves and remaining chopped fresh coriander. Serve at room temperature.

Creamy Asparagus and Pasta Salad

Serves 6-8

INGREDIENTS

250 gm fresh asparagus, trimmed and cut into 2-inch pieces

150 gm farfalle (bow-tie shaped pasta), boiled

200 gm tinned artichoke hearts, cut into bite-sized pieces

1 medium cucumber, sliced

1 cup shredded carrots

2 spring onion stalks, finely chopped

10-12 cherry tomatoes, halved

½ cup thick yogurt

⅓ cup Vinaigrette Dressing (page 202) with 1 crushed clove garlic

Salt to taste

Pepper to taste

Cottage Cheese
Dumpling in
Saffron Gravy
Vilayati Subz Kadai
Tex-Mex Appetiser Tarts

Creamy Quinoa Primavera
Sesame-Crusted Tofu with
Orange-Miso Sauce
Lime Cheesecake Bars
Hot and Sour Tofu Soup

To garnish

Parmesan cheese, as required

Fresh basil leaves, as required

Olive oil, as required

To serve

Melba toast

METHOD

In a shallow dish, pile up first seven ingredients in the order given. Mix together thick yogurt and vinaigrette dressing with crushed garlic, salt and pepper. Drizzle the mixture over the piled up salad. Cover and chill in a refrigerator until ready to serve. Just before serving, toss gently to coat the salad with dressing. Sprinkle cheese, basil leaves and drizzle olive oil. Serve immediately, with melba toast arranged on the rim of the dish.

Creamy Quinoa Primavera

Serves 6-8

INGREDIENTS

1½ cups quinoa, washed and soaked for 20 minutes

3 cups water or thin Vegetable Stock (page 23)

½ cup cream cheese

2 tbsp freshly chopped basil

1 tbsp butter

2-3 cloves crushed garlic

5 cups finely chopped vegetables (asparagus, broccoli, zucchini, peas, carrots etc.)

2-3 tbsp grated Parmesan cheese

To garnish

Chopped nuts, as required

Herbs, as required

Dried cranberries, as required

METHOD

Rinse quinoa thoroughly; drain. In medium-sized pan, heat the quinoa and the stock together. Bring to a boil. Reduce heat; cover and simmer 10 to 15 minutes or until all stock is absorbed.

Stir in the cream cheese and basil; cover and remove from heat and set aside. In a 10-inch non-stick skillet, melt butter over medium heat. Cook the garlic in butter for about 30 seconds, stirring frequently, until golden. Stir in the vegetables.

Cook for about 2 minutes, stirring frequently, until vegetables are tender and crisp. Toss vegetables in the quinoa mixture. Sprinkle with Parmesan cheese. Garnish with chopped nuts, herbs and dried cranberries. Serve warm.

(Image on page 46)

Middle-Eastern Wrap with Tahini Dressing

Serves 4

INGREDIENTS

4 loaves whole-wheat pita bread

½ cup hummus

For filling

1 cup cooked rice

¼ cup toasted pine nuts

¼ cup cubed feta cheese

¼ cup thinly sliced sun-dried tomatoes

½ cup broccoli, chopped and blanched

½ medium red or yellow pepper, diced

1 stalk spring onion, sliced

1 tbsp olive oil

1 tbsp freshly chopped basil

Salt to taste

Pepper to taste

For tahini dressing

¼ cup tahina paste

¼ cup thick yogurt

4 cloves garlic, crushed

2 small green chillies, finely chopped

Juice of 1 lemon

Salt to taste

METHOD

Mix together rice, pine nuts, feta cheese, sun-dried tomatoes, broccoli, pepper, spring onion, olive oil, basil, salt and pepper. Toss gently to mix and keep it in the refrigerator. In another bowl, mix all the ingredients for the tahini dressing. Just before serving, mix the dressing with the rice mixture and toss gently. Warm the pita bread and spread hummus on each one evenly and spoon the mixture and roll up. Serve immediately. Alternatively, you can use lettuce leaves or tortillas instead of pita bread as wrappers

Vilayati Subz Kadai

Serves 6

INGREDIENTS

100 gm peppers, cut into 2-inch cubes

100 gm mushrooms, cut into half vertically

100 gm broccoli, cut into 2-inch cubes

100 gm yellow corn, cut into 2-inch cubes

100 gm French beans, cut into 2-inch cubes

100 gm courgette

2 tbsp sesame oil

1 tsp caraway seeds

1 tsp onion seeds

1 tsp crushed garlic

¼ cup peeled and halved shallots

½ tsp cumin seeds

½ tsp chilli powder

¼ cup peeled and halved cherry tomatoes

½ tsp dried fenugreek leaves (*kasuri methi*)

½ tsp sugar

Salt to taste

Chaat masala to taste

Pepper to taste

To garnish

Slivered ginger, as required

Finely chopped fresh coriander, as required

To serve

Cooked cracked wheat

METHOD

Blanch the vegetables individually in boiling water for 5-7 minutes. In a heavy-bottomed pan, heat oil and crackle caraway and onion seeds.

Add garlic, and shallots. Sauté until soft. Add blanched vegetables, and all the spices. Cook for 2-3 minutes. Add cherry tomatoes, *kasuri methi* and seasoning.

Remove from heat and garnish with ginger and chopped coriander. Serve hot on bed of cracked wheat.

(Image on page 45)

Balti-Style Paneer and Broccoli Curry

Serves 4

INGREDIENTS

1 tbsp oil
½ tsp cumin seeds
½ tsp fennel seeds
1 medium onion, sliced
2 cloves garlic, crushed
1 inch ginger, finely chopped
2-3 tbsp Curry Paste (recipe follows)
250 gm broccoli, separated into florets
500 gm cottage cheese, cut into cubes
4 medium tomatoes, cut into wedges
1 tsp *garam masala*
2 tbsp finely chopped fresh coriander
Salt to taste

METHOD

Heat oil in a wok and fry cumin and fennel seeds until they splutter. Add onion, garlic and ginger. Cook for 5-7 minutes. Stir in the curry paste and cook further for 2-3 minutes. Add broccoli florets and stir-fry for 5 minutes. Add cottage cheese and tomato wedges along with *garam masala* and chopped coriander. Sprinkle little water if the mixture becomes too dry. Cook further for 6-8 minutes. Serve hot with *tandoori roti.*

Curry Paste

Makes 2½ cups

INGREDIENTS

½ cup coriander seeds
4 tbsp cumin seeds
2 tbsp fenugreek seeds
2 tbsp fennel seeds
4 dried red chillies
5 curry leaves
1 tbsp chilli powder
1 tbsp turmeric powder
⅓ cup vinegar
1 cup oil

METHOD

Grind the whole spices to a fine powder. Transfer to a bowl and add the remaining ground spices and mix. Add the vinegar and 5 tablespoons water to form a thin paste. Heat the oil in a large frying pan and add the *masala* mixture. Stir-fry the curry paste for 10 minutes or until all the water has been absorbed. When the oil rises to the surface, the paste is cooked. Allow it to cool. Fill in an airtight jar and cover the top with little more oil and store in cool place. Use as required.

Note: *Balti* cooking is a very popular way of cooking and all-time favourite in the U.K. A simple stir-fry using a shallow wok is all you need to make a quick sumptuous Indian curry.

Cottage Cheese Dumpling in Saffron Gravy

Serves 6-8

INGREDIENTS

For dumplings

500 gm cottage cheese, crumbled
1 tsp chopped green chilli
1 tsp ginger paste
Salt to taste
1 tsp red chilli powder
1-2 tbsp corn flour + for dusting
2 tbsp fresh cream
Oil for deep-frying

For gravy

¼ cup cashew nut paste
200 gm onions, boiled and made into paste
1 tbsp ginger paste
1 tbsp garlic paste
1 tbsp red chilli paste
¼ cup ghee
1 tsp chopped ginger
1 tsp chopped green chillies
1 tsp *garam masala*
¾ cup fresh tomato purée
1¼ cups beaten yogurt
¼ cup cream
½ tsp powdered saffron
Salt to taste

To garnish

Fresh cream, as required
Chopped fresh coriander, as required

METHOD

For the dumplings, mix together cottage cheese, chilli, ginger paste, salt, chilli powder, 1-2 tablespoons corn flour and cream. Make small balls and dust them with corn flour; deep-fry in hot oil over medium heat until golden. Set aside.

For the gravy, mix the pastes of cashew nuts, onion, ginger, garlic and red chilli in a bowl.

Heat the ghee and fry the paste mixture for 2-3 minutes. Add chopped ginger, chillies, *garam masala* and roast till the spices separate from the ghee. Sprinkle little water if necessary. Add tomato purée, bring to a boil and simmer till butter separates again. Add yogurt and cook in the same way.

Mix cream and saffron together in a small bowl and add to the gravy. Bring to a boil and then simmer for 5 minutes. Just before you serve, heat the gravy first and then add the dumplings and simmer for 5 minutes. Pour into serving dish, garnish with a swirl of fresh cream and coriander. Serve hot with *roti*.

(Image on page 45)

Hara Bhara Rice

Serves 4

INGREDIENTS

For rice

4 tbsp ghee
2-3 cinnamon sticks
2-3 cloves
2-3 peppercorns
2-3 cardamoms
2 bay leaves
2 onions, thinly sliced
2 green chillies
200 gm cauliflower or broccoli
200 gm sliced potatoes
½ cup shelled and boiled green peas
1 tsp *garam masala*
Salt to taste
1 cup cooked Basmati rice

For green chutney

1 bunch fresh coriander
4-5 spinach leaves
1 inch ginger
4-5 green chillies
2-3 cloves garlic
1 tsp lemon juice
Salt to taste

To garnish

Finely chopped coriander, as required
Spring onions, as required

To serve

Spiced coconut milk

METHOD

For the chutney, grind together all the ingredients of the green chutney to make a smooth paste in a grinder.

For the rice, heat 1 tablespoon of ghee in a frying pan and fry cinnamon, cloves, peppercorns, cardamoms and bay leaves for ½ a minute. Add sliced onions and green chillies and cook until transparent and set aside. In a wide pan, heat the remaining ghee and fry the vegetables for 4-5 minutes. Add the chutney and cook for 1 minute.

Add fried onion mixture, *garam masala*, salt and rice. Mix well. Transfer rice to a serving dish, garnish with chopped coriander and spring onions and serve hot with spiced coconut milk.

Lime Cheesecake Bars

Makes 24 pieces

INGREDIENTS

For crust

300 gm oatmeal or digestive oats biscuit crumbs

50 gm melted butter

¼ cup powdered sugar

For cheesecake

300 gm Philadelphia cream cheese

200 gm sweetened condensed milk

5 gm China grass mixed with 5 tbsp water or 4 tsp gelatine mixed with 5 tbsp water or liquid

100 gm whipping cream

Juice and grated rind of 2 limes

For topping

¾ cups reserved biscuit crumbs

¾ cups coarsely chopped nuts mixed with sugar

To garnish

Thinly sliced lime

METHOD

For the crust, place biscuit crumbs, reserving ¾ cup for the topping, in a bowl and fold in the melted butter and sugar. Line the base of 13-inch x 9-inch with prepared biscuit crumbs and press with the back of your hand to spread evenly. Bake in preheated oven at 180°C/350°F/Gas Mark 4 for 10 minutes and set aside to cool.

For the cheesecake, place the cream cheese and condensed milk in a blender jar. Process until well blended. Transfer the mixture in a large bowl. Mix China grass or gelatine with water and gently heat it till it is transparent.

Remove it from heat, cool it by stirring constantly. Strain through a fine sieve and fold into the basic mixture gently. Whip the cream until it forms soft peaks, add to the cheese mixture folding in gently.

Add lime juice and grated rind. Pour over the prepared crust. Spread evenly. Chill until set. Remove from refrigerator and top it with mixture of biscuit crumbs and sugared nuts. Garnish with slices of lime. Cut into 1½-inch squares and serve chilled.

(Image on page 46)

Apple Brownies

Serves 8

INGREDIENTS

½ cup butter
1 cup powdered brown sugar
¼ cup thick cream or 1 egg, beaten
½ cup chopped almonds or walnuts
2 medium apples, peeled, cored and finely chopped
1¼ cups refined flour, sieved
½ tsp baking powder
½ tsp soda bicarbonate
½ tsp salt
½ tsp cinnamon powder

To garnish

Cinnamon sugar

METHOD

In a large bowl, beat together the butter and sugar until light. Add beaten egg (if using) or add the cream. Fold in nuts and chopped apples. Mix together refined flour, baking powder, soda bicarbonate, salt and cinnamon powder and fold into the butter mixture.

Transfer the batter into a greased 7-inch x 11-inch baking tin and bake at 150°C/300°F/ Gas Mark 2 for 30-35 minutes. Cool and cut into squares, sprinkle with cinnamon sugar and serve warm.

Coffee Cheesecake Tarts

Makes 12-14 tarts

INGREDIENTS

12-14 tart cases

For cheesecake

1 cup cream cheese
½ cup condensed milk
½ cup whipping cream
2 tsp gelatine powder mixed with 3 tbsp strong coffee
1 tsp Camp coffee essence or vanilla essence

To garnish

Grated chocolate

METHOD

For the cheesecake, in a medium bowl, beat the cream cheese with condensed milk until light. Whip the cream in a separate bowl until stiff. Fold it into the cheese mixture. Cook gelatine powder and coffee mixture on low heat till the gelatine dissolves. Cool.

Place the bowl of cheese mixture over a bowl of ice and add coffee essence and pour the mixture, in a thin stream, into the cheese mixture. When the mixture begins to set, fill in a piping bag and freeze for 5-10 minutes to harden.

Pipe the cheesecake mixture into tart cases and garnish with grated chocolate. Chill the tarts until ready to serve.

Date and Apricot Bars

Makes 24 bars

INGREDIENTS

For filling

1½ cups apricots
1½ cups seedless dates
½ cup white sugar
2 tbsp orange juice
2 tbsp slivered orange peel

For crust

¾ cup melted butter
2 cups plain flour
2 cups quick cooking oats
1 cup brown sugar
1 tsp soda
1 tsp vanilla essence

To garnish

Slivered almonds

METHOD

For the filling, soak apricots in water for 2-3 hours and chop. Chop the dates. Mix together dates, apricots, sugar and orange juice in a pan and cook for 3 minutes or until it reaches the consistency of jam. Remove from heat and cool. For the crust, mix all the ingredients in a bowl and press ½ the mixture in 12-inch x 9-inch x 2-inch greased baking tray. Spread date-apricot mixture evenly over the crust.

Press lightly to make the surface even. Top it with remaining crust mixture, pressing down gently. Bake in preheated oven at 180°C/350°F/Gas Mark 4 for 30 minutes. Remove from oven, sprinkle with slivered almonds and cool slightly. Cut into equal-sized bars.

Fruit and Praline Tart

Serves 10

INGREDIENTS

3-4 cups of fruit of your choice, such as sliced strawberries, sliced peaches, halved green or red grapes, peeled and sliced small bananas, peeled and sliced kiwi and orange

For sweet tart pastry

1½ cups plain flour, sieved
⅛ tsp salt
½ cup butter
¼ cup fresh cream
¼ cup powdered sugar

For pastry cream

1½ cups milk
2 tbsp corn flour
4 tbsp sugar
1 tsp vanilla essence
1 cup whipping cream

For glaze

½ cup raspberry or apricot preserve
2 tbsp warm water
2 tbsp sugar
1 tbsp Grand Marnier (optional)

To garnish

Whipped cream, as required
Praline powder, as required

METHOD

For the tart, preheat the oven to 150°C/300°F/Gas Mark 2. Sieve the flour and salt. In another bowl, beat the butter, cream and sugar until smooth. Blend into the flour. Form a soft ball and press it down on the base and sides of a 9-inch pie dish. Trim the edges. Bake for 20-25 minutes in the oven. Remove and set aside to cool.

For pastry cream, in a pan, mix together milk, corn flour and sugar until well mixed and free of lumps. Heat gently, stirring all the time. Remove from heat when it is thick. Add the vanilla essence. Set aside to cool. Whip the cream until stiff. Fold into the milk mixture. Refrigerate until ready to use.

For the glaze, in a small bowl mix all the ingredients and mix well. Set aside.

Prepare all the fruit as mentioned or cut them as per your liking.

To assemble, spread the prepared pastry cream evenly on the base of the tart. Arrange all the fruits decoratively, alternating with different colours. Spread the glaze evenly and gently over the fruit. Pipe whipped cream to decorate and sprinkle the tart with praline powder and chill until ready to serve.

Barbeque

Spiced Iced Tea Punch

Serves 6

INGREDIENTS

8 tsp black tea leaves

2 tsp Tea Masala (recipe follows)

¾ cup rock sugar, powdered

A handful of lemon grass

A handful of mint leaves

Juice of 2 lemons

To garnish

Lemon slices studded with cloves, slivered ginger, lemon grass stalks, cinnamon sticks, fresh mint leaves and whole cardamoms

To serve

Flavoured ice cubes

METHOD

Bring 4 cups water to a boil in a pan. Remove from heat and add tea leaves, tea *masala* and sugar. Cover and set aside for 2-3 minutes. Remove lid and add lemon grass and mint leaves. Cool to room temperature.

Strain and add lemon juice. Adjust sugar to taste. Pour the mixture into a large punch bowl. Add all the garnishes to the bowl along with some ice cubes.

To serve, place 5-6 ice cubes at the bottom of each glass. Top with chilled tea and serve. Provide straws which can be used as stirrers.

Tea Masala

Grind together 10 grams each of black peppercorns, cinnamon, cloves and dried ginger and 40 grams of whole cardamom to a smooth powder. Store in an airtight container.

(Image on page 64)

Green Pea Parcels

Serves 4-6

INGREDIENTS

1 tbsp oil

1 tsp cumin seeds

500 gm fresh green peas, washed

¼ tsp soda bicarbonate

½ tsp chilli powder

½ tsp salt

To garnish

Finely chopped coriander

METHOD

Heat oil in a frying pan, add cumin seeds. When they change colour add peas and soda bicarbonate. Toss gently till peas are coated with oil. Cook for 4-5 minutes and remove from heat. Take a big piece of foil and transfer the peas in the centre. Sprinkle with chilli powder and salt. Pack the parcel leaving enough space for air to expand. Place under hot grill or on burning charcoal for 7-8 minutes. Open the parcel, garnish with chopped coriander and serve hot.

Barbequed Vegetable Kabab Rolls

Serves 12-14

INGREDIENTS

250 gm potatoes, boiled and mashed

1 cup mixed vegetables, finely chopped and boiled

2 tsp ginger-garlic paste

1 tsp chilli powder

¼ tsp turmeric powder

Salt to taste

¼ cup yogurt, beaten

2 tbsp finely chopped cashew nuts or almonds

½ cup roasted gram flour

Juice of 1 lemon

Oil for frying

12-14 mini oblong bread pieces, slit vertically

To garnish

2 thinly sliced onions, fried

4-5 slices lemon

A few mint leaves

To serve

Barbeque Sauce (page 68), as required

METHOD

Mix together mashed potatoes, vegetables, ginger-garlic paste, chilli powder, turmeric powder and salt. Use potato masher to mix them well. Add yogurt, nuts, gram flour, lemon juice and mix well.

Take about 1 tablespoon of mixture on your palm and roll it into oblong shape about 1½-inch long or to fit the size of bread you are using. Repeat this for the rest of the mixture. Set them aside. Thread them onto skewers and grill them over charcoal on the grill. Remove from skewers and stuff in the warmed bread. Pour 1 teaspoon of sauce, place thinly sliced onions and little mint leaves, close lightly and insert a toothpick to secure and serve warm with lemon slices and additional barbeque sauce.

Note: For a crunchier top, roll each kabab in breadcrumbs and then grill.

(Image on page 63)

Skewered Baby Potatoes and Onions

Serves 4-6

INGREDIENTS

½ kg baby potatoes
¼ kg small onions

For marinade
¼ cup olive oil
2 tbsp lemon juice
1 tbsp dill, finely chopped
2 cloves garlic, minced
Salt to taste
Pepper to taste

METHOD

Cook potatoes in boiling salted water for 10 minutes and drain. Cook onions the same way for 5 minutes. Drain and rinse in cold water. Peel off the skin of each onion. Thread potatoes and onions alternately on skewers. Place in a shallow baking dish.

For the marinade, combine all the ingredients in a screw top jar and shake well. Pour marinade over vegetables and let it stand for 2 hours, turning occasionally. Cook skewered vegetables on an uncovered grill for 10-15 minutes or till tender. To serve, remove vegetables from skewers. Toss with the remaining marinade and serve.

(Image on page 64)

Fruit Kabab

Serves 4-6

INGREDIENTS

1 cup pineapple chunks
12-14 strawberries, washed
2-3 kiwi fruits, cubed
2 large apples, cut into ½-inch cubes
Butter for greasing

For orange baste
½ cup orange juice
2 tsp lemon juice
1 tbsp honey
1 tbsp brandy (optional)
A pinch of cinnamon

To serve
Ice cream of your choice

METHOD

For the orange baste, mix together all the ingredients and place in a wide bowl. Skewer all the fruits onto the skewers. Brush them with baste. Set aside for ½ hour. Barbeque the fruits on a greased grill or griddle, turning them from time to time and brushing them with baste. Serve hot with ice cream of your choice.

(Image on page 64)

Rajma Galouti Kabab

Makes 20-24 kababs

INGREDIENTS

300 gm red or pink kidney beans, soaked overnight

2 tbsp oil + for shallow-frying

1 tbsp ginger paste

1 tbsp garlic paste

2 tbsp chopped cashew nuts

1 tbsp cudpahnuts (*chironji*)

2-3 green chillies, finely chopped

1 tsp caraway seeds

2 tbsp roasted gram flour

2 tbsp *mawa/khoya*

½ cup deep fried onions

1 tsp *garam masala* powder

½ tsp cardamom powder

½ tsp white pepper powder

20-25 fresh mint leaves

Juice of 1 lemon

Salt to taste

To garnish

Thinly sliced onions sprinkled with *chaat masala*

To serve

Mint and Coriander Chutney (page 68)

METHOD

Drain the water in which kidney beans were soaked, add fresh water and cook in pressure cooker till the pressure is released thrice (3 whistles). Remove when cooled, discard extra water and mash them. Heat 2 tablespoons of oil in a wide pan; add ginger-garlic paste, cashew nuts, cudpahnuts, green chillies, caraway seeds and sauté until fragrant. Add roasted gram flour and *mawa*. Cook for 2 minutes.

Add fried onions, mashed kidney beans, *garam masala*, cardamom powder, white pepper powder, mint leaves lemon juice, and salt. Mix well. Allow the mixture to cool slightly. Transfer to a mixer jar and grind to a fine paste. Place in a shallow bowl or a plate and shape into walnut-sized balls and press to a flat round kababs. Place the kababs on a grill, drizzle some oil and cook, turning sides, till golden and slightly crisp. Alternatively, cook them on a hot griddle the same way. Garnish with sliced onions and serve hot with mint and coriander chutney.

Barbequed Vegetables with Vinaigrette Dressing

Serves 6-8

INGREDIENTS

1 kg mixed vegetables (such as mushrooms, peppers cut into strips, slender brinjal, zucchini, asparagus, baby carrots, halved new potatoes, quartered ears of corn, onion wedges)

For vinaigrette dressing

⅓ cup olive oil
3 tbsp wine vinegar
3 cloves garlic, minced
1 tbsp fresh basil, finely chopped
1 tsp rosemary, oregano, sage, thyme or marjoram, crushed
½ tsp salt
½ tsp pepper

METHOD

Combine all the ingredients, for the vinaigrette dressing, in a screw top jar, shake well. Set aside. Arrange vegetables on a greased rack, brush them with the dressing and grill till vegetables are tender brushing frequently with vinaigrette. When cooked, transfer onto a serving plate and pour the remaining dressing and serve at room temperature.

(Image on adjacent page)

Barbequed Corn on the Cob with Cheese-Butter

Serves 6

INGREDIENTS

6 corn on the cob with the husk
100 gm butter, softened
50 gm Cheddar cheese, shredded
2 tbsp spring onions, finely chopped
½ tsp Worcestershire sauce
¼ tsp salt
¼ tsp pepper
¼ tsp chilli powder

Barbequed Corn on the Cob with Cheese-Butter
Barbequed Vegetables with Vinaigrette Dressing
Barbequed Mushrooms with Herbed Cheese
Barbequed Vegetable Kabab Rolls

Spiced Iced Tea Punch
Skewered Baby Potatoes and Onions
Crunchy Coleslaw
Fruit Kabab
Mustard Sauce

METHOD

Pull down a few husks for strands from the corn, rinse the corn and soak for 15 minutes. Meanwhile, for the cheese butter, combine all the remaining ingredients in a mixing bowl. Mix till well-blended and set aside.

Remove corn from the water and cook directly over coal till tender, turning frequently. Remove husks and serve with cheese butter.

(Image on page 63)

Barbequed Moghlai Vegetable with Cottage Cheese

Serves 6-8

INGREDIENTS

500 gm cottage cheese, cut into cubes

250 gm cauliflower, cut into cubes

250 gm pepper, cut into cubes

250 gm onions, cut into cubes

250 gm tomatoes, cut into cubes

For marinade

5 tbsp oil

1 medium onions, grated

2 tbsp ginger-garlic paste (made with 1-inch ginger and 10 cloves garlic)

2 tbsp *tandoori masala*

1 tbsp *garam masala*

Salt to taste

¼ cup tomato purée

4 cups thick yogurt

Chilli powder to taste

To serve

Mint Chutney (page 68) and sliced onions

METHOD

For marinade, heat oil; fry onions till translucent. Add ginger-garlic paste and fry for 1 minute. Add all the spices, salt and tomato purée and fry for 2-3 minutes. Add the yogurt and fry again for 3-4 minutes. Remove from the heat. Add cottage cheese and the vegetables, except the tomatoes, and marinade in a shallow dish for 3-4 hours.

Just before grilling, add the tomatoes and thread the vegetables alternately on the skewers. Roll them generously in the marinade. Cook on a hot grill until the vegetables are tender. Serve with mint chutney and sliced onions.

Barbequed Mushrooms with Herbed Cheese

Serves 6-8

INGREDIENTS

12-14 white mushrooms, stems removed and washed

2 tbsp olive oil

2 tbsp breadcrumbs

3 tbsp toasted and chopped walnuts or pine nuts

For herbed cheese

200 gm cream cheese, softened

2 cloves garlic, freshly crushed with a little salt

1 tbsp freshly chopped mixed herbs

75 gm butter, melted and cooled

METHOD

For the mushrooms, clean the mushroom caps from inside and remove the black bits. Brush them with olive oil, sprinkle some breadcrumbs and place under the grill for 10-12 minutes or until soft but firm. Remove and set aside.

For herbed cheese, in a bowl beat cream cheese with the crushed garlic and the fresh herbs, and then gently fold the cooled melted butter into the mixture. Do not add the butter while hot or the mixture will curdle. Fill this mixture into a piping bag and stuff grilled mushrooms with this mixture. Sprinkle with nuts and serve warm or cold.

Note: Use this cheese mixture to pipe over vegetable pieces like cucumber, tomato, peppers etc.

(Image on page 63)

Barbequed Curry Paste Rice

Serves 4-6

INGREDIENTS

1 cup Thai Jasmine rice or long grain rice

3-4 tbsp sesame oil

2-3 tbsp red or green Thai curry paste

3-4 kaffir lime leaves

3-4 basil leaves

Salt to taste

Sugar to taste

To garnish

2-3 stems spring onions

A bunch of basil leaves

To serve

Coconut Sauce (page 68)

METHOD

Wash and soak rice for ½ an hour. Boil 2 cups of water in a medium-sized pan, add soaked rice and cook briskly. Remove from heat just before it is completely cooked (approx. 7-8 minutes). In another medium-sized pan, heat oil and fry curry paste briefly.

Add cooked rice, Kaffir lime leaves, basil, salt and sugar. Mix well until rice is thoroughly coated with the paste. Turn it out on a piece of foil (approx. 12 inches) and make a tight packet. Place over a hot grill for 4-5 minutes, turning over once in between. Place the packet on a serving plate, garnish with spring onions and basil and serve hot with coconut sauce.

Barbequed Pizza

Makes 8 pizzas

INGREDIENTS

For dough

1¼ cups refined flour or whole-wheat flour

½ tsp salt

2 tbsp dried yeast

2 tsp whole sugar

1 tbsp olive oil + for brushing

For topping

1 cup thick pizza sauce

1 medium onion, finely chopped

1 medium pepper, finely chopped

10-12 basil leaves, finely chopped

200 gm pizza cheese, grated

To serve

Chilli flakes

METHOD

For the dough, sift the flour in a bowl with salt. In a small bowl, take ½ cup lukewarm water and sprinkle yeast and sugar over it. Cover and place in a closed cupboard for 10 minutes. When the mixture is frothy, pour over the sifted flour along with 1 tablespoon olive oil, and knead to make a soft dough. Add a little extra water if required. Cover and set aside for 1-1½ hours in a closed oven or until the dough has doubled in size. Knead the dough and divide into 8 small parts.

Take one portion and with the help of dry flour, roll it into a 3-inch disc. Place this on the barbeque grill and cook for 3-4 minutes. Turn it over and cook for another 2 minutes. Remove from the grill and brush the top with olive oil then spread 1½ tablespoons of thick sauce evenly on the round. Sprinkle with onion, pepper, basil and cheese. Place on the grill again until the cheese melts and serve immediately.

Barbeque Accompaniments

Barbeque Sauce: Fry 2 medium onions, finely chopped in 2 tablespoons olive oil, add 2-3 crushed garlic cloves, and fry for 1 minute. Add 2 cups blanched and chopped tomatoes, 2 tbsp wine vinegar, 2 tbsp brown sugar, 1 tsp pepper, 1 tsp salt, 1 tsp paprika, 1 tsp mustard, ½ tsp Tabasco and 1 tbsp Worcestershire sauce. Simmer this for 30 minutes; purée in a blender and sieve. Serve hot or cold.

Makes 2 cups

Coconut Sauce: Heat 1 tsp sesame oil, add 2-3 each of lemon grass sticks, basil leaves, chopped red chilles and lime leaves. Allow it to sizzle for 1 minute. Add 1 cup of coconut milk, salt and sugar to taste. Remove from stove. Do not boil the sauce or else it will curdle. Serve warm or cold.

Makes 1 cup

Coriander Chutney: Place 1 bunch finely chopped coriander leaves, ½ cup grated coconut, ¼ cup roasted peanuts, 3-4 green chillies, 1-inch ginger, 1 tbsp sugar, ½ tsp cumin seeds, juice of 1 lemon, salt to taste in a small grinder and make a coarse paste. Serve with savoury snacks.

Makes 1 cup

Crunchy Coleslaw: Mix together 1 cup shredded cabbage, 1 medium coarsely grated carrot, 2 finely chopped celery sticks, 1 chopped spring onion, 1 small-sized chopped pepper in a large bowl. Add ¼ cup cracked wheat (which has been soaked in water for ½ an hour) and toss gently. Set aside in the refrigerator. In another small bowl, mix together ½ cup mayonnaise, ¼ cup thick yogurt, 1 tsp salt, 1 tsp sugar, 1 tsp pepper, 1 tsp mustard, and 1 tsp sugar. Toss the vegetables with this dressing and serve cold.

(Image on page 64) *Serves 4*

Mango, Mint and Coriander Chutney: Grind together ¼ kg unripe green mangoes, cut into small pieces, 1 cup mint leaves, 2 cups coarsely chopped coriander leaves, 2 tomatoes, cut into small pieces, 1 medium onion, cut into small pieces, 7-8 green chillies, 1 tbsp sugar, and salt to taste, to make a paste. Add a little water, if necessary. Serve with savoury dishes.

Makes 1 cup

Mint Chutney: Grind together ½ cup fresh coriander, ½ cup mint leaves, 2 tbsp coconut, 2 tbsp roasted grams, 4-5 green chillies, ½-inch ginger, juice of 1 lemon, salt and sugar to taste.

Makes 1 cup

Mustard Sauce: Mix together 1 cup vegetable stock (made with 1 cup water + 1 stock cube), 2 tbsp mustard powder, 2 tbsp fresh cream, 1 tsp dried tarragon leaves, 1 tsp powdered sugar, and 1 tbsp lemon juice in a small pan and bring to a boil. Remove from heat and cool slightly. Fold in 1 cup sour cream, 2 tbsp chopped chives, and salt gently. Serve warm.

(Image on page 64) *Makes 1½ cups*

Kids' Party

Fresh Fruit Punch

Serves 8-10

INGREDIENTS

1 cup rock sugar
1 cup water
2 tbsp lemon juice
1 litre cranberry juice
3 cups chopped mixed fruit (pineapple, melon, strawberries, kiwi and grapes)
A few mint leaves
500 ml soda
Crushed ice

To garnish
Long candy

METHOD

Heat sugar and water in a pan until sugar has melted. Set aside to cool. Add lemon juice and cranberry juice. Toss the fruit with mint leaves. Just before serving, take a stemmed glass, spoon 2 tablespoons fruit mixture at the bottom of the glass, add crushed ice and top it with ½ cup juice mixture and finally top it with soda. Garnish with candy and serve chilled.

(Image on page 81)

Candy Bar Smoothie

Makes 4 glasses

INGREDIENTS

1 cup sweetened condensed milk
1 cup vanilla ice cream
½ cup grated milk chocolate
2 candy bars of your choice (Kit Kat, Twix, Mars etc.)
2 cups crushed ice

To garnish
Whipped cream

METHOD

Combine all ingredients in a blender. Blend until smooth. Pour into tall glasses, garnish with whipped cream and serve.

Nachos Supreme

Serves 4-6

INGREDIENTS

200 gm taco chips
1 recipe Refried Beans (recipe follows)
1 recipe Red Salsa (recipe follows)
1 recipe Nacho Sauce (recipe follows)
½ cup jalapeño chillies

To serve

Sour Cream (recipe follows)

METHOD

To assemble nachos, preheat the oven to 150°C/300°F/Gas Mark 2. Place 12-14 taco chips in an oven-proof baking dish. Pile up refried beans and salsa over each chip. Pour nacho sauce over and arrange sliced jalapeño chillies. Bake for 3-4 minutes and serve right away with sour cream at the side.

(Image on page 82)

Refried Beans *Makes 2-2½ cups*

Cook 200 gm kidney beans (rajma), soaked overnight, in a pressure cooker along with 1 medium onion, coarsely chopped, 2-3 cloves garlic and salt to taste, until soft (3-4 whistles). Remove from the cooker and slightly mash them with a rounded spoon. Return to the heat and cook them again with 1 tbsp taco seasoning mix, 1 tbsp Red Salsa (recipe follows) and 1 tbsp butter. Mix well.

(Image on page 82)

Red Salsa *Makes 1 cup*

Place 4 medium tomatoes, coarsely chopped, 1 medium onion, chopped, 3-4 cloves garlic, 1 tbsp red chilli paste, 1 tbsp vinegar, 1 tbsp chopped fresh coriander, 2 tbsp finely chopped jalapeño chillies, 1 tsp salt, 1 tsp taco seasoning mix, and a large pinch of dried oregano in a blender jar. Blend to make a sauce but take care not to purée it.

(Image on page 82 & 127)

Nacho Sauce *Makes 2 cups*

Mix 250 gm nacho cheese, 1 cup milk, 2 tbsp Red Salsa (recipe above), 1 tbsp finely chopped jalapeño chillies and 1 tsp taco seasoning mix, in a pan and bring to a boil. Remove from heat and set aside to cool slightly.

Sour Cream *Makes 1½ cups*

Mix 250 gm nacho cheese, 1 cup milk, 2 tbsp Red Salsa (recipe above), 1 tbsp finely chopped jalapeño chillies and 1 tsp taco seasoning mix, in a pan and bring to a boil. Remove from heat and set aside to cool slightly.

(Image on page 82 & 127)

Chilli-Garlic Potatoes

Serves 4

INGREDIENTS

2 tbsp soy sauce

1 tbsp vinegar

1 tbsp refined flour

2 tbsp tomato ketchup

2 tbsp oil

Salt to taste

Pepper to taste

250 gm potatoes, parboiled, peeled and cut into 2-inch long sticks or 250 gm baby potatoes, parboiled and peeled

1 tsp red chilli paste

1 tsp crushed garlic

1 green chilli, crushed

½ tsp MSG (optional)

To garnish

2-3 green chillies, slit and finely chopped fresh coriander

METHOD

Mix together soy sauce, vinegar, refined flour, tomato ketchup, 1 tablespoons oil, salt and pepper. Soak potatoes in this mixture for 2-3 hours. Heat 1 tablespoon of oil in a frying pan, fry chilli paste and crushed garlic and crushed chilli along with 2-3 tablespoons of water and cook for 1 minute.

Add soaked potato mixture and MSG (if using). Cook till the sauces dry out. Serve hot with toothpicks as a starter, garnished with slit green chillies and chopped coriander, or just as an accompaniment to your Chinese meal.

(Image on page 81)

Italian Pizza Salad

Serves 6

INGREDIENTS

250 gm uncooked pasta of your choice

1 cup cherry tomatoes, halved

½ cup sliced spring onions

½ cup olives

½ cup pepper

1 cup pizza cheese, cubed

½ tsp Italian seasoning

½ tsp chilli flakes

¼ tsp freshly ground pepper

6-inch round pizza base

For dressing

4 tbsp freshly chopped basil
1 large clove garlic, minced
2 tbsp grated Parmesan cheese
4 tbsp olive oil
2 tbsp lemon juice
Salt to taste
Pepper to taste

METHOD

Boil the pasta for 8-10 minutes, drain and set aside. To make the dressing, mix all the ingredients in a small bowl and whisk until well blended. Pour this over the pasta and toss. Add remaining salad ingredients except the pizza base and toss again. Cover and refrigerate for 2-3 hours.

To serve the salad, halve the pizza base horizontally and brush each half of the cut surface lightly with olive oil. Toast in the oven until crisp. Remove and place on a serving platter. Just before serving, divide the salad into two portions and pile the salad over the pizza bases and serve immediately.

(Image on page 81)

Layered Bean Dip

Serves 8

INGREDIENTS

2 cups finely chopped lettuce
1 tin baked beans
2 medium tomatoes, chopped
1 cup shredded sharp Cheddar cheese
½ cup Sour Cream (page 71)
½ cup ranch dressing
or Mayonnaise (page 202)
1 tsp Worcestershire sauce
1 tsp Tabasco sauce
1 tbsp taco seasoning mix
¼ cup jalapeño chillies
¼ cup sliced spring onion

To garnish

Finely chopped parsley

To serve

Tortilla chips, assorted chips or crackers

METHOD

In a 9-inch pie plate, layer shredded lettuce, beans, chopped tomatoes and cheese. In a small bowl, combine together the sour cream and salad dressing. Add Worcestershire sauce, Tabasco sauce and taco seasoning. Mix well; spoon over cheese layer. Sprinkle with jalapeño and spring onion. Garnish with parsley. Serve bean dip immediately or store, covered, in refrigerator for up to 2 hours. Serve with tortilla chips or assorted chips or crackers.

Tex-Mex Pizza

Serves 4

INGREDIENTS

For dough

½ cup refined flour

½ cup maize flour

A pinch of salt

1 tbsp oil + for brushing

For topping

½ cup kidney beans, soaked overnight and boiled

2-3 tbsp Red Salsa (page 71)

1 tsp taco seasoning

Salt to taste

2 stems spring onions, finely chopped

½ cup grated pizza cheese

METHOD

For dough, mix both the flours and salt in a bowl. Make a well in the centre and add oil. Set aside for 5-10 minutes. Make a soft dough with warm water. Divide the dough into 4 balls. Roll out each one to a thin 6-7-inch disc. Slightly roast it on a dry griddle, brush lightly with oil and set aside.

For topping, preheat the oven for 170°C/325°F/Gas Mark 3. Mash the beans completely. Add salsa, taco seasoning and salt. Mix well. If the mixture feels wet, transfer to a shallow pan and cook until it becomes dry. Set aside to cool.

Just before serving, spread 2-3 tablespoons topping on the prepared tortilla base. Sprinkle with spring onions and cheese. Bake in the oven for 5-7 minutes or until the cheese has melted. Cut into wedges and serve.

Spinach and Tomato Layered Rice

Serves 8

INGREDIENTS

1 tbsp ghee

2-3 cinnamon

2-3 cloves

2-3 cardamoms

2 cups Basmati rice, washed and soaked for ½ hour

For spinach layer

1 tbsp ghee

1 large onion, chopped

2 tbsp finely chopped ginger-green chillies mixture

2 cups spinach leaves, washed, boiled and mashed

1 tsp *garam masala*

Salt to taste

200 gm cottage cheese, cubed

For tomato layer

6 medium tomatoes, blanched and chopped

½ cup fresh cream

Salt to taste

Pepper to taste

Sugar to taste

Chilli powder to taste

To garnish

Sliced and fried onions, fried almonds or cashew nuts

METHOD

Heat ghee in a thick-bottomed pan; add cinnamon, cloves and cardamoms. Fry until fragrant. Add soaked and drained rice and cook until rice grains are coated with ghee. Add water and cook the rice until almost done. Remove and spread rice on a large plate. Set aside.

For spinach layer, heat ghee in a pan and fry onion, ginger–chilli mixture for 1 minute. Add the spinach, *garam masala* and salt. Cook for 1 more minute and add cubed cottage cheese. Remove from heat. Add ½ the rice to this mixture and toss gently to mix.

For tomato layer, mix the blanched tomatoes, cream, salt, pepper, sugar and chilli powder in a bowl. Add remaining rice to this mixture.

Spread the tomato rice layer over the spinach layer evenly. Cover the mould and bake at 200°C/400°F/Gas Mark 6 for 15-20 minutes. Unmould the rice on a serving plate and garnish with fried onions and nuts. Serve hot with yogurt or *kadhi*.

Three Layered Italian Casserole

Serves 6-8

INGREDIENTS

For first layer

250 gm Aglio-Olio Pasta (page 29)

¼ cup cream

For second layer

500 gm vegetables (zucchini, peppers, brinjals, mushrooms, tomatoes, onions)

2 tbsp butter or olive oil

2 tbsp freshly chopped herbs

Salt to taste

Pepper to taste

For third layer

400 gm cottage cheese or Ricotta cheese, crumbled

½ cup fresh cream

2 tbsp Parmesan cheese

2 tbsp chopped parsley

To garnish

Grated mozzarella cheese, chilli flakes and halved cherry tomatoes

To serve

Sliced crusty bread brushed with flavoured olive oil

METHOD

Preheat the oven to 180°C/350°C/Gas Mark 4.

Grease 8 cup-sized casseroles with little butter and layer as following:

For first layer, toss aglio-olio pasta with cream and layer on greased casserole at the bottom.

For second layer, slice chosen vegetables into long strips or round. Place under a grill for 2 minutes. Remove, toss with butter or olive oil, herbs, salt and pepper. Place under the grill for another 5-7 minutes or until slightly charred. Layer these vegetables over the pasta in the casserole.

For third layer, blend together cottage or ricotta cheese with cream and Parmesan in a blender. Transfer to a bowl and fold in the parsley. Add a little milk if you find the mixture too thick. Spread this evenly over the vegetables. Garnish with mozzarella cheese, chilli flakes and cherry tomatoes. Bake in the oven for about 20-25 minutes. Serve hot with crusty bread.

Cake Pops

Makes 24 pops

INGREDIENTS

For pops

½-¾ kg chocolate sponge cake, crumbled

5 cups chopped semi-sweet cooking chocolate

24 lollipop sticks

For cocoa butter-cream frosting

6 tbsp butter, softened

2⅔ cups sieved powdered sugar

½ cup cocoa powder

⅓ cup milk

½ tsp vanilla essence

To garnish

⅔ cup melted white chocolate and colourful sprinkles

METHOD

Mix together all the ingredients for cocoa butter-cream frosting. Place cake crumbs in a bowl, add the frosting to it and beat until well-combined. Using a small ice cream scoop, drop 1½-inch mounds onto waxed paper lined baking sheet. Roll mounds into balls and freeze for 30 minutes.

Place ½ cup semi-sweet chocolate in a small pan and place on low heat until just melted. Remove from heat and cool for 30 seconds. Dip one end of each stick into the melted chocolate and then stick it into each frozen cake balls. Freeze the pops for 30-60 minutes until firm.

In another pan, place remaining semi-sweet chocolate on low heat or microwave just until chocolate has melted. Working in batches, dip the frozen cake pops into the melted chocolate mixture. Allow excess to drip off. When the chocolate is just about to set, drizzle with melted white chocolate and sprinkles. Keep the pops standing on floral foam to dry out completely for approximately 30 minutes. Store in the refrigerator. Let them stand for 30 minutes at room temperature, before serving.

(Image on page 82)

Almond Cookie Fruit Pizza

Makes 20 pieces

INGREDIENTS

For almond cookie

175 gm butter

125 gm powdered sugar

200 gm refined flour, sifted

50 gm ground almonds

1 tsp vanilla essence

2 tbsp orange or pineapple juice

2 cups sliced fresh fruit (kiwi, grapes, oranges)

For topping

200 gm cream cheese

⅓ cup icing sugar

For glaze

½ cup orange marmalade mixed with 2 tbsp water

METHOD

Preheat the oven to 140°C/275°F/Gas Mark 1.

For almond cookie, beat together butter and sugar until light and fluffy. Add flour and almonds to form soft dough. Chill for 10 minutes in the refrigerator. Roll out the dough onto a floured surface into a large disc. Cut into rounds with a 2-inch round cookie cutter. Place on a baking sheet and bake for 20 minutes or until pale golden. Cool on a wire rack.

For topping, in a medium bowl, beat together cream cheese with icing sugar, vanilla essence and juice. Spread 1 tablespoon of mixture on each cookie and then top with sliced fruit. Arrange all the cookies on a serving platter, spread little of the glaze over each one and chill for 30 minutes before serving.

Note: You can roll out the dough in 7-inch discs and make a bigger pizza.

Oreo Trifle

Makes 6-8 bowls

INGREDIENTS

1 packet Oreo cookies, separated and cream removed

200 gm whipping cream

200 gm cream cheese

1 tsp vanilla essence

1 large apple, peeled and sliced

To garnish

Chocolate cigars or curls and whipped cream

METHOD

Coarsely crush the cookies, keeping aside 2-3 for garnishing. Whip the cream to form stiff peaks and set aside. In a medium-sized bowl, beat the cream cheese until light. Fold in whipped cream and vanilla essence. Set aside. Take 6 cup-sized transparent bowl or 6-8 individual bowls. Place few of the Oreo pieces at the bottom of the bowl.

Spread cream cheese mixture evenly. Top it with sliced apple. Repeat the layers once more and pipe the cream on top for garnish. Stick one chocolate cigar diagonally or decorate with chocolate curls. Chill for 3-4 hours.

(Image on page 82)

Chocolate Cupcakes

Makes 14-16 cupcakes

INGREDIENTS

225 gm refined flour
4 tbsp cocoa powder
1 tsp baking powder
½ tsp baking soda
225 gm butter
225 gm powdered sugar
4 eggs
1 tsp vanilla or mint essence
100 gm plain chocolate chips
14-16 paper cup liners

METHOD

Pre-heat the oven to 150°C/300°F/Gas Mark 2. Prepare cupcake moulds with paper liners. Sift together flour, cocoa, baking powder and baking soda. In a medium-sized bowl, beat butter and sugar together until light. Add eggs one at a time beating well after each addition. Reduce beater speed to low and add the flour mixture little at a time.

Add essence and beat to mix. Fold in the chocolate chips in down to upward movement to retain the lightness of the batter. Spoon mixture into paper cups, ¾ full, and bake for 25 minutes. Remove from oven, cool for 10 minutes. Ice or frost the cakes as you like.

Recommended frosting/icing

Chocolate butter cream with mint essence, cream cheese frosting, cappuccino frosting, cocoa glaze.

Frostings and Icings for Cupcakes

Cappuccino frosting

Makes 2 cups

INGREDIENTS

1 cup butter, at room temperature

2¼ cups icing sugar

2 tbsp instant coffee mixed with 2 tbsp water

1 tbsp Camp coffee essence

METHOD

Beat butter until light and fluffy. Add icing sugar little at a time, beating after each addition. When half the sugar is beaten in, add the coffee mixture and coffee essence. Finish by adding the remaining icing sugar. The mixture should look very light and frothy. Fill in a piping bag or syringe and use as required.

Whipped cream frosting

Makes 1¼ cups

INGREDIENTS

1 cup whipping cream

3 tbsp icing sugar

1 tsp flavouring (vanilla essence, cinnamon powder, instant coffee powder, lemon/mint/orange essence)

METHOD

Make sure whipping cream is cold. Transfer cream to a stainless steel bowl and beat with an electric beater to form a soft peak. Add sugar a spoonful at a time. Gently fold in the flavouring of your choice. Place in the refrigerator until ready to use. You may fill in a pipping bag with star nozzle or simply use with pallet knife to frost the cakes.

Note: You can also add ½ cup strawberry purée or 1½ tablespoons sieved cocoa powder as a variation to the flavouring.

Italian Pizza Salad
Chilli-Garlic Potatoes
Fresh Fruit Punch

Cake Pops
Oreo Trifle
Nachos Supreme
with Red Salsa
Refried Beans
Above: Sour Cream

Butter cream frosting

Makes 1cup

INGREDIENTS

½ cup butter, at room temperature
1 cup sieved icing sugar
2-3 tbsp milk
1 tsp vanilla/mint/caramel/ orange essence

METHOD

In a large bowl, beat butter, sugar, milk and preferred essence until smooth. Add additional milk, if necessary, 1 teaspoon at a time until frosting is of the desired spreading consistency. If you wish to use the icing to pipe on the cake it is recommended to keep icing stiff.

Note: For chocolate butter cream frosting, add 2 tablespoons sieved cocoa powder along with sugar. Adjust consistency by adding extra milk.

Cocoa glaze

Makes 1½ cups

INGREDIENTS

2 tbsp butter
¼ cup unsweetened cocoa powder
½ tsp vanilla extract
1¼ cups powdered sugar

METHOD

In a small pan, melt butter over low heat. Stir in cocoa and 3 tablespoons water. Cook, stirring constantly, until mixture thickens. Do not boil. Remove from heat. Stir in vanilla extract. Gradually add powdered sugar, beating with whisk until smooth. Add additional water, ½ teaspoon at a time, until desired consistency is achieved.

Peanut butter frosting

Makes 1¾ cups

INGREDIENTS

3½ cups powdered sugar
¾ cup peanut butter
2 tbsp butter
1½ tsp vanilla essence
1½-3 tbsp milk

METHOD

Beat together powdered sugar, peanut butter, butter, vanilla and enough milk for required consistency.

Cream cheese frosting

Makes 2 cups

INGREDIENTS

225 gm cream cheese
½ cup butter
1 tsp vanilla essence or any other flavour of your choice
450 gm icing sugar
3-4 tbsp milk

METHOD

Place cream cheese and butter in the bowl of an electric beater. Beat on low speed until combined. Add vanilla essence. Gradually add icing sugar. Scrape down beater and bowl. Add milk slowly while beating. Continue beating on medium speed until icing is smooth. Use as required.

Note: Chocolate cream cheese icing can be made by adding 100 gm melted and cooled dark cooking chocolate to the above icing. Chocolate should be added before adding sugar. If the icing gets too stiff more milk should be added to achieve softer consistency.

White chocolate butter cream icing

Makes 3 cups

INGREDIENTS

200 gm white chocolate, cut into pieces
¼ cup fresh cream
1 cup butter
1 cup powdered sugar
1 tsp vanilla essence
½ cup whipping cream

METHOD

Place chocolate and fresh cream in a glass bowl and melt in a microwave oven for 1 minute or until melted or place in a metal bowl over a pan of hot water. Transfer mixture to a large bowl and beat in butter until creamy. Add sugar little at a time. Add vanilla essence. Whip the cream in a separate bowl until soft peaks are formed. Fold gently into chocolate mixture. Use as required.

Additional toppings for Cupcake decoration:

1. Chocolate vermicelli
2. Coloured sugar crystals
3. Gems or Smarties
4. Chocolate cigars
5. Toasted coconut flakes
6. Praline powder
7. Sugar flowers
8. Chocolate shavings or chopped chocolate
9. Orange or lemon peel
10. Candied fruits
11. Coffee bean
12. Slivered almonds

Sunday Brunch

Maiden Mary

Serves 1

INGREDIENTS

1 cup tomato juice
½ tsp Worcestershire sauce
A dash of Tabasco sauce
Salt to taste
Pepper to taste

To serve

Celery stalk, cucumber sticks and ice cubes

METHOD

Mix all the ingredients in a shaker and pour over ice cubes in a Collins glass. Place celery stalk or cucumber stick and serve.

Note: Add 30 ml Vodka per serving for a Bloody Mary.

(Image on page 100)

Coconut Refresher

Serves 4

INGREDIENTS

2 tender coconuts
2 tsp sugar
½ tsp lemon juice
A small pinch of salt
½ cup finely diced apple
Splashes of grenadine syrup

To garnish

A few red rose petals

METHOD

Chill the coconuts in their shells thoroughly. Remove water and the flesh. Blend both together with sugar and lemon juice in a blender till smooth. Add a pinch of salt. Pour into glasses and add apple pieces and splashes of grenadine. Decorate with rose petals and serve.

Prune and Apple Smoothie

Serves 2

INGREDIENTS

6 prunes, pitted and soaked in warm water

1½ cups apple juice

1 cup crushed ice

½ cup yogurt

¾ tsp vanilla essence

¼ tsp cinnamon powder

A pinch of grated nutmeg

METHOD

Drain the prunes. Combine all the ingredients in a blender jar and blend until smooth. Pour into a tall glass and serve.

Potato and Vegetable Pancakes

Makes 20 pancakes

INGREDIENTS

450 gm potatoes, peeled and grated

2 tbsp milk

2 tbsp refined flour

¼ cup grated cheese

1 tsp salt

1 tsp pepper

1 tsp Italian seasoning

1 cup grated carrots

1 cup zucchini

1 tbsp olive oil, for greasing

To serve

Sour Cream (page 71) flavoured with basil and chives

METHOD

Preheat the oven to 220°C/425°F/Gas Mark 7. Wrap the grated potatoes in several layers of tissues; squeeze to remove all liquid. In a bowl, mix together milk, flour, cheese, salt, pepper and seasoning. Add potato, carrot and zucchini; mix together.

Grease 2 baking sheets. Portion a heaped tablespoon of vegetable mixture onto the baking sheets; flatten to make a pancake. Bake them for 10-15 minutes or until bottom is browned. Turn and bake for 5 more minutes. Serve hot with flavoured sour cream.

Kothimbir Vadi Chaat

Steamed and Fried Savoury Coriander Cakes with Yogurt

Serves 4

INGREDIENTS

2 packed cups coriander leaves with stems, finely chopped

1 cup gram flour

¼ cup mixed flour (whole-wheat flour + millet flour)

1 tbsp rice flour

4-5 green chillies, finely chopped

1 tsp ginger-garlic paste

1 tbsp white sesame seeds

1 tsp poppy seeds

1 tsp turmeric powder

1 tsp *garam masala*

1 tsp sugar

¼ tsp asafoetida

¼ tsp soda bicarbonate

Juice of ½ a lemon

Salt to taste

Oil for frying

For chaat

1 cup thick yogurt mixed with 1 tsp sugar

½ cup Sweet and Sour Chutney (recipe follows)

½ cup Green Chutney (recipe follows)

Chaat masala, chilli powder and roasted cumin powder to taste

100 gm thick *sev*

To garnish

Finely chopped fresh coriander

METHOD

Mix all the ingredients for *vadi* in a bowl except the oil. Add little water at a time to make a thick batter. Make sure that you remove all lumps.

Grease a flat-bottomed tin with oil and pour the batter. Steam it using a traditional steamer or pressure cooker without its weight for around 20-30 minutes over a medium heat.

A skewer inserted in the middle should come clean. Allow it to cool completely before you unmould it. Cut it into desired shapes. I cut them into wedges or small squares. You can either serve them as is or fry them. Heat about ½ cm of oil in a pan and arrange these slices. Fry on both sides till they turn golden brown and crisp.

To assemble *chaat*, place 2-3 pieces of *vadi* in a bowl, pour 2 tablespoons yogurt, the chutneys, spice powders, salt, *sev* and chopped coriander. Serve at once.

Sweet and Sour Chutney

Mix together in a pan, ½ cup tamarind pulp, ¾ cup jaggery, ½ teaspoon black salt, ½ teaspoon salt and ½ teaspoon pepper powder, 1 teaspoon cumin powder and 1 teaspoon chilli powder. Bring to a boil and set aside to cool. Makes ¾ cup.

Green Chutney

Grind together 2 cups roughly chopped coriander leaves, 2-3 chopped green chillies, 1-inch ginger, ½ tsp cumin seeds, 1 tsp sugar, 1 tbsp roasted split Bengal gram, juice of 1 lemon and a pinch of asafoetida with a little water to make a smooth paste. Store in the refrigerator. Makes 1 cup.

(Image on page 99)

Mushroom and Tofu Tom Yum Soup

Serves 4-6

INGREDIENTS

2 lemon grass sticks

2 Kaffir lime leaves

2 sliced galangal

Oil for frying

½ cup tofu, cut into equal sized cubes

1 cup fresh mushrooms, washed and cut into cubes or 1 cup mixed vegetables (carrot, cabbage, cauliflower etc.)

3-5 fresh red chillies

1-2 tsp lemon juice

1-2 tsp soy sauce

1-2 tbsp Nam Prig Pud (chilli paste) (recipe follows)

To garnish

Sprigs of coriander and red chillies

METHOD

Bring 1 litre of water to boil in a pan; add the lemon grass sticks, lime leaves and galangal. Boil for 7-8 minutes. Fry tofu in little oil and set aside. Add the mushrooms and vegetables and bring to a boil. Just before serving, add chillies, lemon juice, soy sauce and Nam Prig Pud. Garnish with coriander and red chillies. Serve hot.

Nam Prig Pud

In a small pan, heat ¼ cup oil, add 10-12 shallots, 10-12 garlic cloves, 10-12 dried red chillies. Roast until fragrant. Remove from heat and transfer to a mortar, add 1½ tbsp of raw sugar and 1 tsp salt. Coarsely pound the paste. Add 2-3 tbsp of water while pounding. Transfer the paste to a bowl and add 2 tsp of tamarind paste and 2-3 tbsp water. Fill in a jar and can be stored up to 2-3 weeks.

Makes ½ cup

Mediterranean Potato Salad

Serves 6

INGREDIENTS

4 medium potatoes, boiled and cut into 1-inch pieces
¼ cup finely chopped parsley
¼ cup white onion
¼ cup toasted pine nuts
¼ cup hummus
¼ cup thick yogurt
1 large clove garlic, minced
1 tbsp lemon juice
¼ tsp salt
¼ tsp pepper

To garnish

Chives, chopped spring onions, paprika and olive oil

To serve

Crisp pita wedges

METHOD

Place potatoes in a refrigerator. In a large bowl, mix together the potatoes, parsley, onion, and nuts, reserving 1 tablespoon pine nuts for garnishing. Combine remaining ingredients and gently fold into the potatoes, coating thoroughly. Make a big pile of the salad in the centre of a plate; garnish with chives, spring onions, remaining pine nuts, paprika and olive oil. Serve cold.

(Image on page 100)

Couscous Royale

Serves 6

INGREDIENTS

For couscous

2 cups couscous
1 tbsp chilli flakes
1 tbsp olive oil
1 tbsp freshly chopped herbs
2-3 tbsp olive oil
500 gm vegetables, as per your choice (asparagus, zucchini, peppers, carrots, baby corn etc., cut into 1-inch pieces)
Salt to taste
Pepper to taste
2-3 tbsp fresh herbs

To garnish

Thick balsamic vinegar, chilli sauce and crisp lavash

To serve

Harissa mixed with olive oil

METHOD

Make couscous as per instructions on the packet. While still warm, toss chilli flakes, olive oil and fresh herbs. Set aside. In a frying pan, heat olive oil and sauté prepared vegetables on a high flame for 3-4 minutes. Add salt, pepper and herbs.

To assemble, take a 6-inch stainless steel ring, for a 6-inch plate. Place the ring in the centre of the plate. Place a scoop or scoops of warm couscous and make a flat layer to fill up half the height of the ring, pressing it lightly. Pile up the hot sautéed vegetables over this to come slightly over the rim.

Drizzle balsamic vinegar and chilli sauce around the ring till the rim of the plate. Very gently pick up the ring to form a round torte like layers of couscous and vegetables. Support the lavash by placing it against the torte at an angle. Serve with harissa mixed with oil.

Steamed Semolina Cake

Serves 4-6

INGREDIENTS

250 gm ready-made *rawa idli* mix
1¼ cups sour yogurt
¼ cup boiled peas
¼ cup chopped tomatoes
1 tbsp ginger-chilli paste
2 tbsp chopped coriander
1 tsp ghee, for greasing

For tempering

2 tsp ghee
½ tsp mustard seeds
1 tsp chopped green chillies
A few curry leaves

To garnish

Grated coconut and finely chopped fresh coriander

METHOD

Place the *rawa idli* mix in a bowl, add half the yogurt and mix well. Add the remaining yogurt, peas, tomatoes, ginger-chilli paste and chopped coriander. Grease a 7-inch round mould with 1 teaspoon ghee. Pour the mixture into the mould, cover with a tin foil or a lid and steam over 6-8 cups of boiling water for about 15-20 minutes.

For tempering, heat ghee in a small pan; add mustard seeds. When they splutter, add chillies and curry leaves. Remove the mould from heat, turn it over onto a serving plate and sprinkle the tempering over the steamed cake. Garnish with grated coconut and chopped coriander. Serve immediately.

(Image on page 99)

Green Cottage Cheese Wraps

Makes 4 wraps

Hara Paneer Kathi Rolls

INGREDIENTS

500 gm cottage cheese, cut into strips

2 tbsp oil

2 medium onions, sliced

2 medium tomatoes, finely chopped

4 large Roomali Roti (recipe follows)

A few pieces of charcoal

Salt to taste

For marinade

1 cup chopped spinach leaves

½ cup chopped mint

½ cup chopped coriander

1 inch ginger, chopped

1 tbsp chopped green garlic

3-4 green chillies, chopped

1 tbsp lemon juice

1 tbsp oil

2 tbsp roasted and powdered peanuts

1 tsp *chaat masala*

1 tsp black pepper powder

½ cup grated coconut

Salt to taste

To serve

Green Chutney (page 89) mixed with yogurt

METHOD

For the marinade, place all the ingredients in a blender and blend until smooth. In a shallow dish, place cottage cheese strips and pour the marinade mixture over. Set aside to marinate for 2 hours. In a thick-bottomed frying pan, heat oil, reserving 1 teaspoon.

Add the cottage cheese along with the marinade and cook until all the liquid evaporates, stirring from time to time. If the mixture sticks to the sides, add a little water. Push all the mixture to the sides of the pan. Place burning charcoal in a small metal bowl and place it in the centre of the pan.

Pour the reserved teaspoon of oil over the charcoal and immediately cover the pan tightly with the lid. Keep covered until the coal stops smoking.

Remove the lid and add the onions and the tomatoes and mix. Adjust the salt. Cook briefly till the vegetables wilt slightly. Remove from heat and keep warm.

To assemble the wrap, place one *roti* on a flat surface, spoon 2-3 tablespoons of the cottage cheese mixture in the centre and roll the *roti* up tightly. With a sharp knife, cut each *roti* diagonally into 3-4 pieces or serve whole.

Serve with green chutney mixed with yogurt.

Roomali Roti

Make a dough with 1 cup plain flour, ½ teaspoon salt, 1 tablespoon oil and ⅓ cup warm water. Cover and set aside for 45 minutes. Knead again and divide into 3 parts. Roll out each part into a paper-thin *roti*. Invert a heavy cast iron pan over a gas flame and spread the *roti* on it. Cook for 45 to 50 seconds. Remove, use immediately or fold into a triangle and cover with a piece of muslin.

(Image on page 99)

Potato and Cheese Au Gratin

Serves 8-10

INGREDIENTS

900 gm potatoes (wafer variety)
Salt to taste
Pepper to taste
A pinch of nutmeg
1 tbsp olive oil, for greasing
100 gm Gouda or Cheddar cheese, grated
2 tbsp fresh cream
1 medium onion, roughly chopped
½ cup finely chopped fresh parsley
1 cup milk
1 tbsp butter

To garnish

Sprig of parsley

METHOD

Wash and scrub the potatoes and peel them. Slice them thinly with a wafer slicer and dip them in water until ready to cook. In a small bowl, prepare the seasoning mix by mixing together salt, pepper and nutmeg. Set aside.

Grease 6-inch x 8-inch baking dish with olive oil. Layer sliced potatoes alternately with cheese and seasoning mix, finishing with potato layer. In a small blender jar, place cream, onion, parsley and seasoning mix to taste. Mix well and slowly add the milk while the motor is running.

Pour this mixture over potatoes, dot with butter and bake in a hot oven at 150°C/300°F/ Gas Mark 2 or 170°C/325°F/Gas Mark 3 for 40 minutes. Remove and allow it to rest for 5 minutes, garnish with sprigs of parsley and serve hot as an accompaniment to main dish.

Burmese Khow Suey

Serves 8

INGREDIENTS

2 onions
8 garlic cloves
1 tbsp ginger
4 tbsp oil
½ tsp turmeric powder
½ chilli powder
1½ tbsp curry powder
3-4 tomatoes, cut into small pieces
500 gm chopped and boiled mixed vegetable (cauliflower, carrots, French beans, green peas, and potatoes)
1 tbsp corn flour
1½ cups thin coconut milk
Salt to taste
1 cup thick coconut milk
1 tbsp finely chopped fresh coriander
200 gm spaghetti or egg noodles

To garnish

Wheat Strips (recipe follows)
100 gm potato straws
6 spring onions, finely chopped
3 onions, cut long and deep-fried
4-5 tbsp garlic, chopped and deep-fried
1 tbsp finely chopped fresh coriander

To serve

Soy sauce and chilli sauce

METHOD

Grind to a paste the onion, garlic and ginger. Set aside.

Heat oil in a large pan; fry the onion-ginger-garlic paste for 5 minutes. You could add a little water to prevent it from sticking to the pan. When all the water evaporates, add turmeric, chilli and curry powders. Fry for 7-8 minutes more making sure it doesn't stick. Add tomatoes and mix well.

Next, add the boiled mixed vegetables and mix it so all the vegetables are coated well with the spices. Mix corn flour with ¼ cup water.

Add the corn flour mixture to the thin coconut milk. Add the coconut milk and salt to the vegetable mixture. Cook gently, stirring occasionally until thick.

Add the thick coconut milk and fresh coriander. Boil spaghetti in salt water, drain and put under running cold water, drain again and keep warm until ready to serve. You can serve this dish in a large bowl for a party or in the individual bowls. Place the warm spaghetti in a bowl, pour hot curry over it.

Sprinkle wheat strips and potato straws on it. Garnish with chopped onions, garlic, chopped coriander. Serve with soy sauce and chilli sauce.

Wheat strips

Combine 1½ cups whole-wheat flour, 2 tbsp oil, ½ tsp salt and 1 tbsp sesame seeds with water and make a dough. Divide into 3-4 pieces. Roll the dough pieces into very thin rounds and cut into long strips. Deep-fry in oil till crisp; drain on absorbent paper. Crush into smaller pieces while serving.

Chocolate Almond Torte

Serves 10

INGREDIENTS

200 gm semi-sweet cooking chocolate, chopped

150 gm butter

½ cup refined flour, sieved

½ tsp soda bicarbonate

1 tsp baking powder

A pinch of salt

1 cup finely ground almonds

1½ cups sweetened condensed milk

¼ cup milk

½ tsp vanilla essence

To garnish

Slivered almonds, icing sugar and whipped cream

METHOD

Preheat the oven to 190°C/375°F/Gas Mark 5. Line an 8-inch round tin with greaseproof paper or foil. In a medium-sized bowl, melt chocolate and butter together. Sift the flour with soda bicarbonate, baking powder and salt. Toss the flour with ground almonds and set aside.

In another bowl, beat condensed milk with cooled chocolate mixture, milk and vanilla essence until well combined. Fold in the flour mixture little at a time. Pour this in the prepared tin and bake in preheated oven for 35-40 minutes. If a toothpick inserted comes out clean indicates the torte is done.

As soon as you remove the torte from the oven, place slivered almonds around the edge and the centre. Allow the cake to cool in the pan. Lift up the cooled cake with the help of foil or paper and place it on the wire rack.

The cake will rise during baking but fall during cooling, leaving a crisp and cracked crust. Remove the foil or greaseproof paper and place on a serving plate. Dust with icing sugar and garnish with whipping cream. Serve at room temperature or cold.

Chocolate and Praline Gâteau

Serves 8-10

INGREDIENTS

1 (7-inch) chocolate sponge cake

For chocolate cream

100 gm chocolate, broken into pieces

3 tbsp butter

⅔ cup fresh cream

3 tbsp powdered sugar

For praline cream

125 gm butter

¾ cup fresh cream

4 tbsp Praline (recipe follows), powdered

Grated rind of ½ orange

To garnish

3 tbsp icing sugar

3 tbsp praline powder

3 tbsp thinly sliced almonds

METHOD

Cut the cake into half horizontally and set aside. For the chocolate cream, place the chocolate in a bowl over hot water until melted. Add butter and stir till melted. Set aside to cool slightly. Whip the cream and powdered sugar until thick and then fold into the lukewarm chocolate until smooth and shiny. Set aside.

To make the praline cream, beat the butter until light. Whip the cream until thick, then add to the butter a little at a time, mixing gently. Fold in the praline and the orange rind. Place bottom part of the sponge cake on a serving plate and spread with the chocolate cream.

Top with another slice and spread praline cream. Sprinkle icing sugar, praline powder and sliced almonds to garnish. Let it set in the refrigerator until use. Slice vertically and serve chilled.

Praline Powder

Gently heat three-fourth cup of whole sugar in a thick-bottomed pan. Add half a cup of cashew nuts or almonds. Cook until the mixture is rich brown in colour. Remove from the heat and spread the mixture on a baking tray. Set aside to cool. Coarsely powder when completely cold. Store in an air-tight jar.

Makes 1 cup

Blueberry Trifle

Serves 8

INGREDIENTS

8-inch plain sponge cake
1 cup whipping cream
150 gm Mascarpone cheese
1 tsp vanilla essence
2-3 tbsp powdered sugar
2 tbsp Grand Marnier or orange juice
1 tin (440 gm) blueberry topping

To garnish

Crushed ginger or oatmeal cookies and slivered almonds

METHOD

Cut the cake into ½-inch thick slices according to the size of a deep transparent glass serving bowl or 4 individual glasses that you want to use and set aside.

Whip the cream until thick. Soften Mascarpone cheese slightly and add to the cream along with vanilla essence and sugar. Beat until soft peaks form.

To assemble trifle, place cake slices at the bottom of the bowl or a glass. Soak the slices with orange juice or Grand Marnier.

Spread blueberry topping over the cake. Place a large dollop of Mascarpone/cream mixture, levelling the surface. Repeat the layers once or twice depending on the size of the bowl.

Cover and refrigerate for 4 hours or over night. Just before serving, sprinkle with cookie crumbs and slivered almonds. Decorate with piped cream. Serve cold.

Date and Walnut Bread

Serves 8

INGREDIENTS

1 cup refined flour sifted before measuring
2 tsp baking powder
1 tsp soda bicarbonate
1 tsp cinnamon powder
A pinch of salt
6 tbsp powdered sugar
3 tbsp butter, softened
1½ cups chopped black dates
¼ cup fresh cream
½ cup toasted and chopped walnuts

To serve

Butter

METHOD

Sieve together flour, baking powder, soda bicarbonate, cinnamon and a pinch of salt.

Set aside. Mix sugar, butter and dates in bowl. Pour ½ cup hot water over it and set aside for 10 minutes. Add the cream when cooled.

Gently fold in the flour and add walnuts. Pour this mixture into an 8-inch square tin or 7-inch loaf tin. Bake in moderate oven at 180°C/350°F/Gas Mark 4 for 40 minutes.

Remove and cool on a wire rack. When cold, slice and serve with butter.

(Image on adjacent page)

Green Cottage
Cheese Wraps
Candied Walnut
Date and Walnut Bread
Green Chutney
Steamed Semolina Cake

Baked Saffron Sandesh
Mediterranean Potato Salad
Maiden Mary

Baked Saffron Sandesh

Serves 8

Saffron-flavoured Cottage Cheese Dessert

INGREDIENTS

350 gm soft cottage cheese, crumbled

3 tbsp sugar

½ litre milk

1 tin (400 gm) condensed milk

½ tsp powdered cardamom

A few threads of saffron

½ cup chopped nuts (almonds, cashew nuts and pistachios)

To garnish

Edible silver foil or silver dust

METHOD

Place crumbled cottage cheese in a bowl; Heat 1 cup water and sugar in a pan and boil until a thick syrup is formed. Add hot syrup to the cottage cheese, mix well and pour into 6 cup-sized glass casserole, set aside.

In another pan, boil milk and add condensed milk. Mix well. Remove from heat, add cardamom and saffron. Mix well.

Pour this over the cottage cheese mixture. Smoothen the top surface. Bake in a hot oven at 190°C/375°F/Gas Mark 5 or 180°C/350°F/Gas Mark 4 for 20 minutes. Remove from oven; sprinkle the nuts and press them down gently.

Garnish with silver foil or silver dust. Serve warm or cold.

(Image on adjacent page)

Lemon-Ginger Frozen Yogurt with Fresh Fruit Compote

Serves 8

INGREDIENTS

¾ cup sugar
¼ cup corn flour
1 cup whipping cream
2 cup thick yogurt
2-4 tbsp lemon juice
2 tsp finely grated fresh ginger
1 tsp grated rind of lemon or orange

For fruit compote

4 cups freshly chopped fruit of your choice
¼ tsp cinnamon powder
¼ tsp corn flour
½ cup sugar
2 tbsp wine vinegar

To garnish

Caramelised fruit, dried fruit or ginger and mint leaves

METHOD

Mix sugar, corn flour and ¼ cup water in a pan and heat gently till sugar dissolves. Boil for 2 minutes. Remove from heat, strain into a medium-sized bowl and set aside to cool. Refrigerate if required. Whip the cream until soft peaks are formed. Set aside.

In another bowl, whisk the yogurt with wire whisk, add lemon juice, ginger and lemon or orange rind. Add the cooled corn flour mixture. Fold in the whipped cream. Pour into a decorative bowl and freeze until almost set.

For compote, mix all the ingredients together in a thick-bottomed pan, heat very gently until all the ingredients are incorporated properly.

Remove from heat and cool. Pour over frozen yogurt, just before serving. Garnish with candied fruit and mint leaves.

High Tea

Pineapple-Mango Cocktail

Serves 6

INGREDIENTS

2 cups chopped ripe mangoes
½ cup white rum
4 cups pineapple juice
Ice cubes, as required

To garnish

Slices of any tropical fruit such as star fruit, mango, or pineapple

To serve

Ice cubes and 6 highball glasses

METHOD

Purée mangoes, rum and ½ cup water in a blender. Pour ¼ cup purée into each glass. Fill with ice cubes (2-3 in each glass). Top it with pineapple juice (approx. ⅔ cup). Garnish with fruit slices and serve chilled.

(Image on page 117)

25 Toast Toppers

INGREDIENTS

2 loaves French bread, cut into ¼-inch thick slices
¼ cup melted butter or olive oil

METHOD

Preheat the oven to 180°C/350°F/Gas Mark 4. Brush each slice of bread with butter or olive oil and bake in the hot oven for 10-15 minutes or until slightly golden. Use these toasts for the following toppers of your choice.

Toast Toppers

1. Spread ricotta cheese and top it with slices of roasted red pepper and sprinkle with salt, pepper and dried oregano.
2. Rub a roasted garlic clove on the bread and top it with chopped tomatoes which are tossed with salt, pepper and freshly chopped basil.
3. Spread pesto sauce and sprinkle with Parmesan and chopped pine nuts.

4. Spread pesto sauce and top it with slivered sun-dried tomatoes and sliced olives.
5. Spread cream cheese and sprinkle with freshly chopped herbs.
6. Spread with yogurt and hummus mixed; and top it with olive oil and zatar spice mix.
7. Spread with hummus and top it with olive tapenade.
8. Combine ¼ cup mayonnaise with 1 teaspoon wasabi paste, spread on toast and top it with slice of cucumber or radish.
9. Spread Gorgonzola or Manchego cheese and top it with walnuts.
10. Sauté finely chopped mushrooms in butter with salt and thyme. Spread on toast and top it with Parmesan cheese.
11. Spread Brie or any other strong cheese on toast and top it with caramelised onions.
12. Spread thin layer of mayonnaise, sprinkle salt and pepper, place a slice of Cheddar cheese and top it with boiled or tinned asparagus tips.
13. Spread grainy mustard and top it with a piece of lettuce and sliced tomato and cube of cheese.
14. Toss Romaine lettuce squares with Caesar dressing and place it on toast and top it with grated Parmesan.
15. Spread green chutney and top it with a thin slice of boiled potato and sprinkle salt and pepper.
16. Spread mashed avocado and top it with chopped jalapeño and tomato. Sprinkle salt and pepper.
17. Mix crumbled cottage cheese with finely chopped onions, tomato, coriander and green chillies, add salt and pepper. Spread this on toast and grill for 2-3 minutes.
18. Spread cream cheese, top it with sliced cucumber and sprinkle with finely chopped dill, salt and pepper.
19. Spread with crumbled feta cheese and top it with chopped basil and sliced olives.
20. Spread toast with crumbled cottage cheese and top it with chopped celery, red pepper and sprinkle with salt and pepper.
21. Mix little olive oil with dried oregano, chilli flakes, garlic salt and pepper. Spread on toast and top it with Parmesan and grill for 1 minute.
22. Spread green chutney and top it with tomato slice and sprinkle grated cheese, salt and pepper.
23. Spread wasabi paste or spicy mayonnaise, sprinkle black and white sesame seeds and top it with toasted seaweed.
24. Spread thin layer of mayonnaise mixed with mustard and top it with slice of boiled egg and dot with tomato ketchup.
25. Spread grainy mustard, top it with alfa-alfa sprouts and sprinkle with salt, pepper and drizzle a little olive oil.

(Image on page 117)

Seven Layered Mexican Dip

Serves 6-8

INGREDIENTS

Refried Beans (page 71), as required
Red Salsa (page 71), as required
½ cup thinly sliced spring onions
½ cup thinly sliced black or green olives
¾ cup grated Monterey Jack cheese
Guacamole (recipe follows), as required
Sour Cream (page 71), as required

To garnish

Sliced jalapeños and taco seasoning mix

To serve

Tortilla chips choice (flavour of your choice)

METHOD

To assemble, take a 8-9-inch round pie dish and layer all the ingredients in the order given above, up to grated cheese. Now place the dish under a grill until the cheese has melted. Remove and wait for 3-4 minutes.

Spread one layer each of guacamole and sour cream. Garnish with jalapeño slices and sprinkle with taco seasoning. Serve immediately with tortilla chips.

Guacamole

Makes 1 cup

INGREDIENTS

1 ripe avocado
2-3 tbsp lemon juice
Salt to taste
1 tbsp fresh coriander, chopped
2-3 chopped green chilies or jalapeños
2 cloves garlic, mashed
2-3 tbsp minced onion
1 tomato, peeled, seeded and chopped
1 tbsp Mayonnaise (page 202)

METHOD

Cut and mash the avocado with a fork while blending in the lemon juice. Add salt, fresh coriander, green chillies, garlic, onion, tomato and mayonnaise. Mix thoroughly and chill. Serve chilled with tortilla chips.

Asparagus Mousse Puffs

Serves 6-8

INGREDIENTS

250 gm puff biscuits, halved and toasted

For mousse

1 tin (425 gm) green or white asparagus tips

1 tbsp gelatine

1 stock cube, crumbled

¾ cup grated Cheddar cheese

2 tbsp cream cheese

2 tbsp Mayonnaise (page 202)

2 cloves garlic (optional)

Salt to taste

Pepper to taste

Mustard to taste

200 gm fresh cream

To garnish

Freshly chopped chives, chopped fresh asparagus tips

METHOD

For the mousse, drain the asparagus tips and reserve the liquid. Soak gelatine in ¼ cup of the liquid along with stock cube. Cook gently until melted. Set aside to cool. Place asparagus tips, both the cheese, mayonnaise, garlic (if using), salt, pepper and mustard in a blender. Blend until smooth.

While the motor is running, slowly add cooled gelatine mixture, making sure each addition is absorbed well. Turn it out in a large bowl.

Beat the cream over ice until thick. Fold it into asparagus mixture and refrigerate for 5-10 minutes until semi set. Fill this mixture in a piping bag with star nozzle and pipe stars on each piece of puff biscuit. Garnish with chives and asparagus tips. Serve at once.

Avocado Cups

Makes 16 cups

INGREDIENTS

4 slices bread
2-3 tbsp melted butter
¼ tsp mustard
1 tsp + 2 tbsp lemon juice
Salt to taste
2 medium avocados, peeled and mashed
½ cup thick yogurt
1 tbsp crushed garlic
1 tbsp chopped chives
1 small tomato, blanched, seeded and chopped

METHOD

Preheat the oven to 180°C/350°F/Gas Mark 4. Trim the crust of the bread and cut each slice into 4 pieces. Mix the melted butter with mustard, 1 teaspoon lemon juice and a pinch of salt. Spread this mixture on each square. With your index finger, lightly press the squares into miniature muffin cups. Bake for 10-15 minutes. Remove from the oven and set aside to cool. When completely cold, unmould and store in an airtight container.

Sprinkle 2 tablespoons lemon juice over the mashed avocado. Add the remaining ingredients. Mix well and chill in a refrigerator for 1-2 hours. Just before serving, spoon the avocado mixture into the toasted cups and serve.

(Image on page 117)

French Onion Toast

Serves 4-6

INGREDIENTS

2 tbsp butter
2 tbsp olive oil
6 medium onions, thinly sliced and halved
2 tsp powdered sugar
Salt to taste
Pepper to taste
250 ml white wine or Vegetable Stock (page 23) or 150 ml of each mixed together
4-6 (½-inch thick) slices baguette
Mustard to taste
100 gm grated Gruyère cheese

METHOD

Melt butter and oil in a heavy-bottomed frying pan, add onions and cook gently for 20 minutes, tossing occasionally until soft. Add sugar, salt and pepper and cook for a further 10 minutes until golden brown. Increase the heat and add the wine or stock and allow to bubble for 1 minute, reduce heat and cook for 5 minutes or until liquid is absorbed.

Heat the grill or the oven and toast the bread slices. Spread mustard evenly on each one. Pile the onions on top and scatter with cheese. Place under the grill for 1-2 minutes, until golden brown. Serve hot.

Tofu and Vegetable Sandwich

Serves 4

INGREDIENTS

8 slices brown or whole-wheat bread
½ cup thick yogurt
½ cup soft silken tofu
1 tbsp olive oil
1 tbsp low fat butter
1 tbsp finely chopped basil
1 tbsp finely chopped chives
1 tsp garlic salt
1 tsp mustard
1 tsp pepper
1 cup finely grated carrot, onions, cabbage and pepper

To garnish

Sliced tomatoes, olive oil and red chilli flakes

METHOD

Remove crust from the bread slices and cut them into two triangles. Wrap them in damp cloth and set aside. Blend together the yogurt and tofu. Set aside. In a bowl, mix together oil, butter, basil, chives, garlic salt, mustard and pepper. Mix well.

Add all the vegetables and yogurt-tofu mixture. Divide the mixture into 8 equal portions. Spread each portion on 8 triangles.

Cover with the other triangles and lightly press down. Cut each sandwich into half and arrange them on a serving plate.

Cut tomato slices into half and place each half on the halved sandwiches. Drizzle little olive oil and sprinkle red chilli flakes on top and serve.

(Image on page 118)

Chocolate Chip and Almond Cookies

Makes 32 cookies

INGREDIENTS

250 gm refined flour, sieved
2 tsp baking powder
¼ tsp soda bicarbonate
¼ tsp salt
175 gm powdered sugar
125 gm softened butter
250 gm chocolate chips
50 gm roasted and chopped almonds
1 tsp vanilla essence
Milk for binding dough

METHOD

Preheat the oven to 180°C/350°F/Gas Mark 4. Sieve together refined flour, baking powder, soda bicarbonate, salt and sugar. Place in a bowl, add the butter and rub with your fingertips. Gather the dough and add chocolate chips and almonds. Add vanilla essence and a little milk to bind to a stiff dough.

Drop rounded spoonfuls of the dough 2-inch apart onto baking tray for a natural look or roll into walnut-sized balls and press gently to flatten.

Bake in preheated oven for 20-25 minutes or until golden. Remove from oven and place on a rack to cool completely. Store in an air-tight jar.

(Image on page 118)

Orange and Walnut Flapjacks

Makes 12 pieces

INGREDIENTS

250 gm butter, cut into pieces
250 gm powdered brown sugar or caster sugar
175 gm golden syrup
425 gm cooking oats
50 gm walnuts, cut into pieces
Finely grated rind of 1 large orange
3 tbsp finely cut orange marmalade

METHOD

Preheat the oven to 180°C/350°F/Gas Mark 4. Generously butter a 12-inch x 4-inch shallow baking tin. Melt the butter, sugar and golden syrup over a medium heat, stirring continuously. Take off the heat and stir in the oats, walnuts and orange zest. The mixture should be quite soft.

Tip the mixture into the baking tin and level it off. Bake for around 30 minutes or until the edges are golden brown but the centre is still a little soft.

Remove from the oven and mark into 12 pieces while it is still warm, cutting down halfway through the mixture with a sharp knife. Leave to cool.

Heat the marmalade with 1 tablespoon water until it becomes syrupy. Brush this glaze over the flapjack mixture and leave to cool before cutting into 12 pieces. They will keep in an airtight tin for up to a week.

Blue Cheese and Hazelnut Shortbread

Makes 30 shortbread

INGREDIENTS

1 cup crumbled blue cheese (at room temperature)

½ cup butter (at room temperature)

1 cup refined flour

½ cup corn flour

⅔ cup toasted hazelnuts, finely chopped

½ tsp coarse salt

½ tsp pepper

To serve

Truffle-flavoured cream cheese, chopped black olives and balsamic vinegar

METHOD

Preheat the oven at 190°C/375°F/Gas Mark 5. Mix together crumbled cheese and butter in a bowl and beat with electric beater until creamy. Set aside. Mix refined flour, corn flour, hazelnuts, salt and pepper in a small bowl.

Mix this dry mixture into cheese mixture to form a moist dough. Shape the dough into a rectangle, wrap in cling film and refrigerate for an hour. Cut into desired shape and place on baking sheet. Bake for 15 minutes in the centre of the oven. Bake until golden brown at the bottom. Remove and cool on wire rack.

To serve, place a few shortbreads on a serving platter, put a small dollop of truffle-flavoured cream cheese, and sprinkle with chopped black olives and balsamic vinegar and serve.

Date and Walnut Scones

Makes 10-12 scones

INGREDIENTS

2 cups refined flour, sieved
¼ cup powdered sugar
2 tsp baking powder
¾ tsp salt
½ tsp soda bicarbonate
¼ cup chilled butter, cut into cubes
¾ cup milk
½ cup finely chopped dates
¼ cup finely chopped walnuts
⅓ cup buttermilk

For glaze

2 tbsp cold water mixed with
1 tbsp salad oil

To serve

Jam and Clotted Cream (recipe follows)

METHOD

Preheat the oven at 190°C/375°F/Gas Mark 5. Mix the first five ingredients together in a bowl. Then add the butter cubes. Mix this with a sharp knife while cutting through the flour. The mixture should resemble breadcrumbs.

Add milk and mix well. Fold in the dates and walnuts into the mixture with a metal spoon. Finally add the buttermilk to make a firm dough. Transfer the dough onto a floured surface and knead briefly. Pat the dough until ¾-inch thick round. Cut into 2-inch circles with a cookie cutter.

Place the scones on a greased baking tray 2 inches apart from each other. Brush each scone with prepared glaze and bake in the hot oven for 25-30 minutes or until golden brown. Serve hot or cold with jam and clotted cream.

Clotted cream

Makes 1½ cups

INGREDIENTS

1 cup fresh cream, at room temperature
⅓ cup sour cream, at room temperature
1 tbsp icing sugar

METHOD

An hour before serving, pour fresh cream into a bowl and whip it until soft peaks form. Whisk in the sour cream and sugar and continue to beat until the mixture is very thick. Chill until ready to serve. This keeps it fresh for about 4-6 hours.

Apple and Almond/ Walnut Cupcakes

Makes 8-10 cupcakes

INGREDIENTS

½ cup butter
1 cup powdered brown sugar
1 egg, beaten or ¼ cup apple purée or ¼ cup fresh cream
½ cup chopped almonds or walnuts
2 apples, peeled, cored and finely chopped
1¼ cups refined flour, sieved
½ tsp baking powder
½ tsp soda bicarbonate
½ tsp salt
½ tsp cinnamon powder

To garnish

Cinnamon sugar or
Cappuccino frosting or cinnamon cream
Slivered almonds and cinnamon powder

METHOD

Preheat the oven at 180°C/350°F/Gas Mark 4. In a large bowl, beat butter and sugar until light. Add beaten egg (if using), or apple purée or the cream. Fold in nuts and chopped apples.

Mix the remaining ingredients in another bowl and fold them in the butter mixture. Scoop with large-sized ice cream scoop and fill in the greased cupcake moulds or individual paper or silicone cups.

Bake in the hot oven for 20-25 minutes or until golden on top. Cool and set aside, sprinkle with cinnamon sugar and serve warm or frost them with cappuccino frosting and garnish with slivered almonds and cinnamon powder. Serve at room temperature.

Red Velvet Cupcakes

Makes 12 cupcakes

INGREDIENTS

1½ cups refined flour, sieved
½ tsp baking powder
¼ tsp salt
6 tbsp butter
1 cup powdered sugar
2 tbsp red food colour
2 tbsp cocoa powder
¾ cup buttermilk
1 tsp vanilla essence
1 tsp vinegar
½ tsp soda bicarbonate

To garnish

Cream Cheese Frosting (page 84)

METHOD

Preheat the oven at 180°C/350°F/Gas Mark 4. Sieve together the flour, baking powder and salt together in a bowl and set aside. Beat butter and sugar until fluffy. Make a paste with 2 tablespoons water, red food colour and cocoa.

Add the food colour mixture to butter-sugar mixture. Mix well. Gently fold in the flour mixture. One at a time, add buttermilk and vanilla essence and mix well. Mix vinegar and soda bicarbonate in a small bowl and fold it into the cake batter making sure it is incorporated properly.

Using an ice cream scoop, or rounded spoon fill the cupcake moulds with the mixture. Bake in preheated oven for 15-20 minutes. Remove from oven and cool for 10 minutes and then remove from moulds. Frost with cream cheese frosting when completely cool.

Almond and Dried Fruit Tarts

Makes 24 small tarts

INGREDIENTS

100 gm almonds, soaked and peeled

60 gm powdered sugar

A pinch of saffron powder

For dried fruit mixture

¼ cup powdered pistachio or cashew nuts

¼ cup powdered sugar

½ tsp powdered cardamom

1-2 tbsp thick cream

METHOD

Grind almonds to a very fine paste. Mix sugar and almond paste in a heavy-bottomed pan. Cook this mixture stirring constantly. Make sure the mixture doesn't stick to the pan. Cook until the mixture forms a soft lump and leaves the sides of the pan. Remove from heat, add saffron and allow it to cool slightly. Shape the almond paste into tarts by hand or using tart moulds. Allow it to cool in a dry place or refrigerator until set.

For dried fruit mixture, mix together the powdered pistachio, powdered sugar and cardamom in a bowl. Add just enough cream to make a thick paste. Makes ½ cup.

To assemble, stuff the tarts with the mixture and serve.

Chocolate-Hazelnut Fudge

Makes 800 gm

INGREDIENTS

400 gm condensed milk

½ cup milk

200 gm dark cooking chocolate, chopped

2 tbsp maple syrup or honey

200 gm butter

200 gm chopped hazelnuts

METHOD

Mix together condensed milk, milk, chopped chocolate and maple syrup in a heavy-bottomed pan and place over medium heat. Keep stirring from time to time.

Bring to a boil and continue cooking till it reaches a soft lump consistency (approx. 12-15 minutes).

Avacado Cups
Assortment from
25 Toast Toppers
Creamy Pesto
Yogurt and Hummus
Spread
Sun-dried Tomato
and Almond Spread
Black-Olive Tapenade
Cream Cheese with
Herbs
Tomato and Chilli
Mayo
Pineapple-Mango
Cocktail

Creamy Pistachio Bars
Tofu and Vegetable Sandwich
Chocolate Chip and Almond Cookies

Remove from heat, add butter and set aside to cool for 5 minutes without stirring. Then beat the mixture with wooden spoon till it reaches a thick and creamy consistency. Add chopped nuts and mix well.

Pour the mixture into greased 8-inch x 6-inch rectangular tin and cool completely. Cut into desired shapes and sizes and place them in small paper cups. Store in an air tight container.

Creamy Pistachio Bars

Makes 30 pieces

INGREDIENTS

For base

32 Oreo cookies, crushed to crumbs

6 tbsp melted butter

For pistachio cream

½ cup pistachios, blanched

2 tbsp sugar

3-5 tbsp milk

For custard cream

1 cup cold milk

4 tbsp sugar

4 tbsp custard powder

1 cup whipping cream

To garnish

Coarsely chopped pistachios and toffee bits

METHOD

For base, mix together cookie crumbs and butter until well blended. Press onto the bottom of 13-inch x 9-inch pan. Refrigerate until ready to use.

For pistachio cream, roast pistachios in a moderately hot oven until crisp. Take 2 tablespoons pistachios and chop them coarsely. Place remaining pistachios in a small blender jar along with sugar and 3 tablespoons milk. Blend until smooth. Transfer to a bowl and add remaining milk to get a creamy consistency. Chill for 10 minutes.

For custard cream, mix together milk, sugar and custard powder in a pan and heat gently, stirring continuously. Cook until thick. Remove and place over ice water until completely cool. Whip the cream until stiff. Divide the cream into 2 parts. Add one part to pistachio cream and the other to the custard.

Spread pistachio cream evenly over the Oreo crumbs base. Freeze for 10 minutes. Remove and spread custard cream over pistachio cream. Refrigerate until set. Garnish with chopped pistachio and toffee bits. Cut into even sized squares and serve chilled.

(Image on adjacent page)

Petit Fours

Makes 14-16 pieces

INGREDIENTS

For sponge cake

140 gm refined flour, sift before measuring

1½ tsp baking powder

½ tsp soda bicarbonate

4 tbsp melted butter

200 gm sweetened condensed milk

1 tsp vanilla essence

½ cup slivered almonds (optional)

For filling

1 cup apricot jam or orange marmalade

For glaze

1 cup icing sugar

Food colour, as required

To decorate

Sugar flowers or chocolate rice

METHOD

Preheat the oven at 200°C/400°F/Gas Mark 6.

Sieve the flour, baking powder and soda bicarbonate together in a bowl. Set aside. Grease and dust a 13-inch x 9-inch Swiss roll tin. Mix the remaining ingredients along with 5 tablespoons hot water in a bowl and beat with an electric beater.

Fold in the flour mixture into the prepared mixture, little at a time. Pour this mixture into the greased tin and bake in the preheated oven for 10-15 minutes. Remove from oven and cool for 2-3 minutes and invert on a wire rack and cool. Makes ¼ kg sponge cake.

For filling, mix the jam or marmalade with 2-3 tbsp warm water in a small bowl until softened.

For glaze, place icing sugar in a bowl and gradually add 2-3 tablespoons warm water, beating well, until icing is smooth and coats the back of a spoon. Add a few drops of colour and mix well.

To assemble petit fours, cut the cake horizontally into half, and place on the wire rack. Spread jam or marmalade evenly on the surface of the bottom half. Sprinkle with slivered almonds. Cover with another piece of sponge cake, cut side down, pressing firmly together. Cut lengthwise into equal strips and then width wise to form small rectangular pieces. Separate the pieces and place them little apart on the rack.

Pour prepared glaze over each piece, allowing excess icing to fall out. Leave it to dry for 15-20 minutes. Decorate with sugar flowers or chocolate rice.

Cocktail Party

Red Grape Granita

Makes 6 glasses

INGREDIENTS

⅓ cup rock sugar
1 inch cinnamon
2 tbsp lemon juice
500 gm red grapes, seeded and chopped
¾ cup red wine (optional)
6-8 whole grapes
Sugar, as required

METHOD

Combine sugar, ⅓ cup water and cinnamon stick in a pan and bring to a boil, stirring until sugar dissolves. Remove from heat, add lemon juice and cool slightly. Place the grapes and sugar-lemon mixture in a blender jar and purée. Transfer the purée to a rectangular metal pan. Cover and freeze for several hours. Using fork, scrape granita down the length of pan, forming icy flakes. Pour 2 tablespoons wine into each of 6 wide glasses. Roll whole grapes in sugar and set aside. Spoon scraped granita in each glass. Garnish with sugared grape and serve.

Pineapple, Lychee and Mint Daiquiri

Makes 4 glasses

INGREDIENTS

2 cups fresh pineapple, diced
1 cup lychee juice or 5-6 fresh lychees
¼ cup sugar
¼ cup lemon juice
10-12 mint leaves
2-3 cups crushed ice

To garnish

Pineapple leaves

METHOD

Place all the ingredients in a liquidiser jar. Blend until the mixture has the consistency of shaved ice. Pour into cocktail glasses and garnish with pineapple leaves.

(Image on page 128)

Strawberry-Kiwi Sangria

Serves 6-8

INGREDIENTS

4 strawberry flavoured teabags
1 cup sugar
3 kiwi fruit, peeled and cubed
750 ml apple juice
6-8 dried rose petals or ½ teaspoon rose water
2 cups strawberry juice
2 cups ice cubes

METHOD

Bring 2 cups of water to a boil and add the teabags. Remove from heat, cover and set aside for 10 minutes. Discard teabags and add the sugar and another 2 cups of water to the hot tea. Refrigerate for 2-3 hours. Place the chopped fruit in a large pitcher and pour the tea over. Add the remaining ingredients. Stir and serve in stemmed glasses.

(Image on page 128)

Candied Walnuts

Makes 2 cups

INGREDIENTS

2 cup walnut halves
2 tbsp butter
¾ cup sugar
2 tbsp toasted sesame seeds

METHOD

Preheat the oven to 180°C/350°F/Gas Mark 4 and toast the walnuts for 7-8 minutes. Remove and toss walnuts with butter. Place sugar in a medium, heavy-bottomed pan and cook over high heat, stirring, only if required, until it turns a light caramel colour or for 4 to 5 minutes.

Add sesame seeds and the nuts, a few at a time and stir to coat evenly with the mixture. Line a baking sheet with parchment paper. Place coated nuts on the prepared sheet and arrange in a single layer. Allow to cool completely before serving. Store in an airtight jar.

(Image on page 99)

Savoury Cheesecake with Sun-dried Tomato Pesto

Serves 10

INGREDIENTS

For crust

1 cup whole-wheat biscuit crumbs
1 tbsp melted butter
½ cup chopped walnuts or almonds
Salt to taste
Pepper to taste

For pesto

100 gm sun-dried tomatoes, soaked in hot water
1 large clove garlic
¼ cup Parmesan cheese
3 tbsp toasted pine nuts
Salt to taste
Pepper to taste
¼ cup olive oil
1 cup fresh basil leaves, finely chopped

For filling

200 gm cottage cheese
200 gm cream cheese
200 gm Sour Cream (page 71)
1 tsp Worcestershire sauce
2 cloves garlic
Salt to taste

To garnish

Cherry tomatoes, chopped spring onion and boiled corn

To serve

Crackers or melba toast

METHOD

For crust, in a medium bowl, mix together biscuit crumbs, butter and nuts along with salt and pepper to taste. Press this onto loose-bottomed tin and bake in the oven at 170°C/325°F/Gas Mark 3 for 7-8 minutes. Set aside to cool.

For pesto, in a small grinder, grind soaked sun-dried tomato, garlic, Parmesan, pine nuts, salt, pepper and olive oil until smooth. Transfer to a bowl and fold in chopped basil. Add additional olive oil to acquire spreading consistency.

For filling, in a large blender jar, blend together all the ingredients for the filling until very smooth. Transfer to a bowl and set aside.

To assemble, spread half of the cheese mixture filling over baked crust. Spread evenly. Spoon pesto over cheese mixture, levelling with back of a rounded spoon. Cover with remaining cheese mixture. Chill in the refrigerator for 2 hours or until set. To remove the cheesecake from pan, slightly loosen the sides and push the base upwards and slide it on serving platter. Garnish with cherry tomatoes, spring onion and corn in alternate circles. Keep in refrigerator until ready to serve. Place prepared platter on large plate and surround it with crackers and melba toasts.

Asparagus Pizzetta

Makes 12 mini pizzas

INGREDIENTS

10-12 small pizza bases, brushed with olive oil

500 gm fresh asparagus tips, cut into ½-inch pieces

1 tsp basil

1 tsp thyme

1 tsp garlic salt

½ cup Mayonnaise (page 202)

¼ cup cream cheese spread

½ tsp salt

½ tsp pepper

½ tsp mustard paste

2-3 tbsp grated Parmesan cheese

2-3 tbsp pizza seasoning

To garnish

Sliced cherry tomatoes

METHOD

Slightly crisp the pizza bases in the oven. Blanch the asparagus tips in salted boiling water until tender crisp. Drain and place in a bowl. Toss with basil, thyme and garlic salt. In another bowl, mix together mayonnaise, cheese spread, salt, pepper and mustard paste.

Take 1 teaspoon of the above mixture and spread on each pizza base. Place 1 tablespoon of asparagus mixture on top and level it slightly. Sprinkle with cheese and pizza seasoning. Garnish with slices of cherry tomatoes and bake in a hot oven at 180°C/350°F/Gas Mark 4 for 5-7 minutes. Serve warm.

Tandoori Broccoli and Red Peppers

Serves 6-8

INGREDIENTS

250 gm broccoli florets
250 gm red peppers

For marinade

½ cup thick yogurt
1 tsp Bengal gram flour
1 tsp chilli powder
1 tsp cumin powder
2 tbsp ginger-garlic paste
½ tsp dried fenugreek leaves (*kasuri methi*)
1 tbsp *tandoori masala*
1 tbsp mustard oil
2 tsp *chaat masala*
2 tbsp finely chopped coriander
Salt to taste

To garnish

Onion rings and mint leaves
Chaat masala to sprinkle

To serve

Toothpicks or skewers

METHOD

Prepare the marinade by mixing all the ingredients in a shallow dish. Wash and cut broccoli into florets and peppers into cubes. Soak both the vegetables in the prepared marinade for 1 hour.

Thread the vegetables alternately on to skewers and place on charcoal or under electric grill for 10-12 minutes, turning from time to time. Serve hot on the bed of onion rings and mint leaves. Sprinkle some *chaat masala* if you wish.

(Image on adjacent page)

Red Salsa
Sour Cream
Cheese and Jalapeño Poppers
Tandoori Broccoli and Red Peppers
Three-Coloured Cottage Cheese Nibbles

Strawberry-Kiwi Sangria
Pineapple, Lychee and Mint Daiquiri
Herbed Nuts

Olive Poppers

Makes 24 pieces

INGREDIENTS

1 tbsp olive oil
2 cloves garlic
1 tsp chilli flakes
24 pieces whole-stuffed olives

For coating
1 cup sieved refined flour
½ cup butter
2 tbsp grated Parmesan cheese
Salt to taste
Ice cold water

METHOD

Heat oil slightly, add garlic and chilli flakes. Toss olives and set aside.

For the coating, in a small bowl, mix together flour, butter, Parmesan and salt. Add ice cold water if the mixture is too dry. Pull out a little dough, press it with your thumb to form 1½-inch disc and wrap it around one olive. Press gently to seal the olive. Repeat for the rest of the olives. Place them on baking tray and bake in the oven at 170°C/325°F/ Gas Mark 3 for 12-15 minutes or until slightly golden. Serve warm.

Herbed Nuts

Makes 1 cup

INGREDIENTS

1 cup hazelnuts, toasted
2 tbsp butter + olive oil
¼ tsp dried oregano
¼ tsp thyme
¼ tsp chilli flakes
A pinch of cumin powder
Salt to taste
Pepper to taste

METHOD

Chop nuts coarsely. In a frying pan, melt butter. Add the hazelnuts and the rest of the ingredients and sauté until the nuts are well coated with the spices. Remove from heat and set aside to cool. Store in an air tight container.

(Image on adjacent page)

Cheese and Jalapeño Poppers

Makes 16 servings

INGREDIENTS

1 cup shredded Monterey Jack and/ or Cheddar cheese

½ cup diced jalapeño chillies

¼ cup refined flour

Salt to taste

1 tsp taco seasoning mix

Breadcrumbs to roll

Oil for deep-frying

To serve

Sour Cream (page 71)

Red Salsa (page 71)

METHOD

Combine cheese, jalapeño chillies, flour, salt and taco seasoning mix in a medium bowl. Shape like thick chillies or cone shapes. Add little milk if you find the mixture little dry. Roll each one in breadcrumbs and deep-fry in hot oil. Serve with sour cream and salsa.

(Image on page 127)

Feta Cheese Medallions

Makes 14 medallions

INGREDIENTS

200 gm hard feta cheese

¼ cup olive oil

¼ cup breadcrumbs

¼ cup powdered hazelnuts

1 tsp ground black pepper

To serve

Salted crackers

METHOD

Cut the cheese into 1-inch x ½-inch slices. Dip each slice in olive oil, coating well on both sides. In a small bowl, mix together breadcrumbs, hazelnut and pepper.

Roll cheese in this mixture and place on non-stick or slightly greased baking tray (you can refrigerate at this point for several hours or overnight). Bake for 5-6 minutes and serve immediately, either by itself or on a cracker.

Vegetable Crisps with Pepper Cream Dip

Serves 8

INGREDIENTS

For dip

2 large red and yellow peppers, roasted and peeled

2-3 cloves garlic, roasted and peeled

1 tbsp fresh thyme

⅓ cup thick yogurt or Labneh (page 14)

1 tbsp lemon juice

1 tbsp sumac

1 tsp salt

1 tsp sugar

¼ cup olive oil

200 gm cream cheese or crumbled feta cheese

1 tbsp freshly chopped herbs of your choice

To serve

Vegetable chips, tortilla chips and small transparent glasses

METHOD

Combine all the ingredients except cream cheese and herbs in a blender jar and process until smooth. Transfer to a bowl and chill for 30 minutes. In a small bowl, mix together cream cheese and herbs and set aside.

To serve, take a small transparent glass; place 4-5 chips on one side standing up. On the other side of the glass put a dollop of pepper dip. With a smaller scoop place cream cheese over pepper dip and serve at once.

Note: This is served in individual glasses for convenience.

Three-Coloured Cottage Cheese Nibbles

Serves 4

INGREDIENTS

250 gm grated cottage cheese
100 gm grated sharp Cheddar cheese
2 tsp finely chopped parsley
Salt to taste
Pepper to taste
½ cup finely chopped toasted mixed nuts
3 tbsp freshly chopped herbs (chives, parsley, marjoram)
2 tbsp mild paprika

METHOD

Mix together both the cheeses, parsley, salt and pepper and toss to mix well. Shape the mixture into small balls, cover and chill for 20 minutes. Slightly toast chopped nuts and cool.

Sprinkle nuts, herbs and paprika in 3 separate small bowls. Divide cheese balls into 3 equal parts. Roll one parts into nuts, second into herbs and third into paprika. Arrange on a serving platter. Cover with cling wrap and chill until ready to serve.

(Image on page 127)

Celebration Dinner

Christmas Punch

Serves 8

INGREDIENTS

1 litre raspberry or cranberry juice, chilled

750 ml sparkling wine or sparkling red grape drink

½ cup orange juice or orange liqueur, chilled

Juice of 2 large lemons or limes

2 cups fresh fruits (strawberry, blueberry, raspberry, chopped apple and pineapple etc.)

¼ cup mint leaves, plucked and washed

To serve

A large punch bowl

METHOD

Pour the chilled juices in a punch bowl and stir to combine. Add all the fruits, chopped or whole. Garnish with mint leaves. Serve chilled.

(Image on page 146)

Autumn Apple Punch

Serves 12

INGREDIENTS

2 cinnamon sticks

8 cloves

6 cups apple juice

1⅓ cups pineapple juice

¼ cup lemon juice

½ cup orange juice

600-700 ml ginger ale

To garnish

Apple slices, cinnamon sticks

To serve

1 big block of ice, punch bowl

METHOD

Wrap cinnamon stick and cloves in a small piece of muslin and tie with a thread (*potli*). Immerse the *potli* in a pan with apple juice. Simmer uncovered for 20 minutes. Remove from heat; discard the *potli* and set aside to cool slightly.

Mix apple juice with other juices and chill in a refrigerator. Just before serving, take a punch bowl, place block of ice in it and pour the juice over it. Top with ginger ale. Garnish with apple slices and cinnamon sticks. Serve cold.

Corn Rasam

Serves 6

INGREDIENTS

1 tbsp ghee or oil
8-10 black peppercorns
1½ tsp cumin seeds
3-4 dried red chillies, roasted
2-3 pinches cinnamon-clove powder
1 tbsp *rasam* powder
Salt to taste
2 tsp tamarind paste
1 tsp jaggery or ½ tsp sugar
2 large tomatoes, blanched
1 large corn on the cob, grated
½ tsp mustard seeds
¼ tsp asafoetida
2 cloves garlic, chopped
4 cups thin *dal* water
A few curry leaves

To garnish

Finely chopped coriander and grated coconut

METHOD

Heat ½ teaspoon ghee or oil and roast peppercorns and 1 teaspoon cumin seeds till aromatic, grind in a processor till powdered. Add red chillies, cinnamon-clove powder, *rasam* powder, salt, tamarind and jaggery.

Blend all this with tomatoes and grated corn to a thick pulp. In a medium-sized pan, heat remaining ghee; add mustard seeds and remaining cumin seeds, asafoetida and allow it to splutter. Add garlic and stir in the tomato mixture.

Add thin *dal* water, curry leaves and check spices and salt. Simmer for 3-4 minutes. Garnish with chopped coriander and coconut and serve hot in bowls along with a meal or in small glasses as an appetiser.

Paan Shots

Makes 3 shots

INGREDIENTS

6 fresh beetle leaves
2 tsp rose petal jam (*gulkand*)
1 tsp aniseed
A pinch of powdered cardamom
A pinch of *paan masala*
6-8 cubes crushed ice
1 large scoop vanilla ice-cream

To garnish

Beetle nut shavings

METHOD

Blend all the ingredients in a blender until smooth. Pour into shot glasses, garnish with beetle nut shavings and serve immediately.

Sun-dried Tomato and Feta Cheese Puffs

Makes 30-35 pieces

INGREDIENTS

100 gm sun-dried tomatoes
½ cup feta cheese, crumbled
¼ cup finely chopped parsley
3 tbsp chopped green olives
2 tbsp olive oil
2 tbsp Parmesan cheese
1-2 cloves garlic, minced
250 gm puff pastry
Butter to brush and refined flour to roll

METHOD

Preheat the oven at 180°C/350°F/Gas Mark 4. Soak sun-dried tomatoes in boiling water for 15 minutes. Drain and chop them. Combine all the ingredients, except the puff pastry, in a bowl. Mix well until well combined.

Cover and set aside. Roll out puff pastry on a floured surface to 10 mm thickness. Cut into 2½-inch squares. Take 1 square, apply little water on the edges, place 1 teaspoon of tomato mixture and fold over to form a triangle. Press the edges with a fork to seal. Prick with fork in the centre to allow heat to escape.

Brush with melted butter. Place on an oven tray, ½-inch apart. Bake in the hot oven for 20-25 minutes or until golden. Serve warm.

Mediterranean Turnovers

Makes 12-14 appetiser portions

INGREDIENTS

1 tbsp olive oil

1 tbsp crushed garlic

1 tbsp chopped basil

1 tbsp parsley

Salt to taste

Pepper to taste

Chilli flakes to taste

½ cup sun-dried tomatoes, soaked and chopped

½ cup crumbled feta cheese

¼ cup toasted and chopped walnuts

12-14 flour and herb wrappers

½ cup black Olive Tapenade (recipe follows)

To serve

Sour Cream (page 71)

METHOD

Preheat the oven to 180°C/350°F/Gas Mark 4. In a medium bowl, mix together olive oil, crushed garlic, herbs, salt, pepper and chilli flakes. Mix well with a fork. Add sun-dried tomatoes, feta cheese and walnuts. Toss gently with a fork to mix. Take one wrapper; apply 1 teaspoon olive tapenade, spreading evenly. Spoon sun-dried tomato mixture on half of the wrapper and fold over the other half, sealing the corners. Repeat for the remaining wrappers. Place on a baking tray and bake in the hot oven for 4-5 minutes. Remove from oven and serve with sour cream.

Olive Tapenade

Combine 200 gm black olives, 2 tbsp pine nuts or walnuts, 2 tbsp capers, 1 tsp dried oregano, 1 large clove garlic, ½ tsp lemon juice, 2 tbsp virgin olive oil, a pinch of chilli flakes, salt and pepper in a food processor but make sure to retain a coarse texture. Transfer to a jar and store in the refrigerator.

Makes 1 cup

Creamy Salsa Tostadas

Makes 12-14 tostadas

INGREDIENTS

12-14 two-inch round flat taco shells
1 cup Sour Cream (page 71)
½ cup cream cheese
½ cup Red Salsa (page 71)

To garnish
Shredded lettuce and chopped jalapeños

METHOD

Mix sour cream and cream cheese in a bowl and whisk until smooth. Fold in salsa gently making sure to drain out excess water in the salsa. Spoon this mixture onto each tostada, garnish with lettuce and jalapeños. Serve immediately.

(Image on page 146)

Asparagus and Sweet Corn Cakes

Serves 6

INGREDIENTS

3 tbsp butter
250 gm fresh asparagus, trimmed and chopped
500 gm mashed potatoes
⅓ cup boiled or tinned corn kernels
¼ cup milk mixed with 1 tsp corn flour
1 tbsp Mayonnaise (page 202)
1 tbsp chopped parsley
1 tbsp chives
Salt to taste
Pepper to taste
1 cup breadcrumbs
Oil for shallow-frying

To serve
Herb mayonnaise

METHOD

Heat butter in a frying pan and sauté asparagus until tender. Add mashed potato, corn, milk, mayonnaise, herbs, salt and pepper. Remove from heat and allow it to cool. Divide the mixture into 6-8 balls.

Flatten like a patty. Roll it in little milk and dip it in a bowl filled with breadcrumbs. Shallow-fry in hot oil; serve with herb mayonnaise.

Note: To make herb mayonnaise, mix together mayonnaise, fresh herbs, lemon juice, mustard, salt and pepper.

Buttermilk Mozzarella Puffs

Serves 8

INGREDIENTS

For buttermilk biscuit dough

⅓ cup cream

½ cup buttermilk

1 cup sieved self-rising flour

1 tbsp powdered sugar

1 tsp ranch or buttermilk dressing mix

3 tbsp cold butter

For puffs

½ tbsp melted butter, for greasing

100 gm mozzarella cheese, cut into cubes

1 tsp oregano

¼ cup pizza sauce

METHOD

For dough, beat together cream and buttermilk with a whisk. Sift together flour, sugar and buttermilk dressing mix. Cut cold butter into small cubes and rub them into the flour to resemble coarse cornmeal.

Stir in cream and buttermilk mixture until the dough resembles cottage cheese. Sprinkle some flour on a board and turn out the dough. Sprinkle some more flour on the dough and shape them into small balls.

For puffs, preheat the oven at 190°C/375°F/Gas Mark 5. Lightly grease the baking sheet with melted butter. Divide the dough into 8 to 10 parts depending on how big you want the puffs to be.

Gently roll them with your hand and make an indent in the centre of each part. Fill each indent with mozzarella cube, rolled in oregano. Pinch the dough around the cube, and place the pinched side down, on a baking sheet. Cover with pizza sauce and bake in the hot oven for 10-12 minutes or until golden brown.

Cottage Cheese Puffs

Makes 14-16 puffs

INGREDIENTS

For puffs

1 cup refined flour, sifted
½ cup ghee
Salt to taste
½ tsp lemon juice
2 tbsp melted butter for sealing
Oil for greasing
Some milk for brushing

For stuffing

2 tbsp oil
1 large onion, finely chopped
1 tsp mustard paste
2 small green chillies, chopped
½ tsp turmeric powder
1 tsp chilli powder
1 large green pepper, finely chopped
200 gm crumbled cottage cheese
Salt to taste
1 tsp cumin powder
1 tsp coriander powder
1 tsp *chaat masala*
4 tbsp finely chopped coriander leaves

To garnish

Sprig of coriander

To serve

Chilli sauce

METHOD

For puffs, knead together the refined flour, ghee, salt, lemon juice and 3-4 tablespoons cold water, to make a dough. Cover the dough with a damp cloth and set aside for at least 30 minutes.

For stuffing, preheat the oven to 180°C/350°F/Gas Mark 4. Heat the oil in a pan, add onion and cook until transparent. Add mustard paste, green chillies, turmeric and chilli powders, mix well and then add pepper.

Cover and cook for 2-3 minutes. Uncover and add cottage cheese, salt, cumin and coriander powders, *chaat masala* and mix well. Add chopped coriander and remove from heat. Set aside to cool.

Make even-sized balls of the prepared dough and dust in a little flour and flatten them with rolling pin. Cut into 3-inch squares. Brush the edges with little melted butter and place 1 tablespoon cottage cheese stuffing in the centre. Fold them diagonally to form triangles. Press lightly on the edges to seal. Use a fork to seal further by pressing with the tines of the fork. Repeat for the remaining dough.

Grease the baking tray with oil. Arrange the puffs on the tray leaving ½-inch space between them. Brush some milk on top and bake in preheated oven for 20-25 minutes or until brown.

Flip the puffs once in between to bake from both sides. Place 1 puff in a serving plate on one side and make a swirl with chilli sauce and place a sprig of fresh coriander.

Serve hot.

Steamed Lentil Cups

Makes 12-14 cups

INGREDIENTS

½ cup split black-eyed peas (*chawli dal*), soaked overnight

½ cup finely chopped spinach

½ cup fenugreek leaves

2 tbsp chopped dill

1 tbsp ginger-chilli paste

½ tsp asafoetida

Salt to taste

1 tbsp oil

1 tbsp lemon juice

1 tsp fruit salt

To garnish

Freshly chopped coriander and grated coconut

To serve

Green Chutney (page 89)

METHOD

Make a smooth paste of the split peas and add all the three greens, ginger-chilli paste, asafoetida and salt. Mix well. Fill up ⅓ of a large pan with water and bring to a boil. Place a metal plate over the water with ring underneath.

Prepare the silicone or metal cups and arrange over the plate. In a small bowl, mix together 1 tablespoon hot water, oil, lemon juice and fruit salt. Mix, using your fingers and quickly pour on to the lentil batter. Mix well stirring the spoon clockwise. Quickly spoon the mixture into the cups.

Cover the pan and allow them to steam for 7-8 minutes. Remove from heat and cool slightly. Unmould from the cups and garnish with the chopped coriander and coconut. Serve hot with green chutney.

Spicy Roasted Nuts

Makes 1 cup

INGREDIENTS

½ cup cashew nuts

½ cup peanuts, without skin

For black spice

1 tsp oil

1 tsp black salt

1 tsp pepper

1 tsp dried mango powder

For red spice

1 tsp oil

1 tsp salt

1 tsp red chilli powder

1 tsp dried mango powder

1 tsp cumin powder

METHOD

Preheat the oven to 110°C/225°F/Gas Mark ¼. Roast both the nuts separately in the oven for 30 minutes.

For black spice, heat oil in a pan, add cashew nuts. Sprinkle black salt, pepper, dried mango powder all over and mix well until all the nuts are coated well. Cool and store in airtight bottle.

For red spice, heat oil in a pan and add the peanuts. Sprinkle salt, red chilli powder, dried mango powder and cumin powder all over until nuts are coated well. Cool and store in airtight bottle.

Tawa no Handvo

Pan-fried Savoury Cake

Serves 6-8

INGREDIENTS

2 cups Handva Atta (recipe follows)
1 cup sour yogurt
1 tsp sugar
1 cup grated bottle gourd (see note below)
Salt to taste
2-3 tsp ginger-chilli paste
½ tsp soda bicarbonate
A pinch of asafoetida
2 tbsp oil + for greasing
1 tsp fruit salt
1 tsp lemon juice

For tempering

4-5 tbsp oil
1 tsp mustard seeds
2 tsp sesame seeds
A pinch of asafoetida
3-4 dried round red chillies
A few curry leaves

To serve

Green Chutney (page 89) or sweet and sour pickle

METHOD

Soak *handva atta* with sour yogurt and sugar for 6 hours or overnight. Add grated bottle gourd, salt, ginger-chilli paste, soda bicarbonate, asafoetida, 2 tablespoons oil and the fruit salt mixed with a little lemon juice and mix well. Place in the refrigerator.

For the tempering, in a small pan, heat 4 tablespoons oil; add mustard and sesame seeds. When they splutter, add asafoetida, red chillies and curry leaves. Set aside. Heat a small frying pan; coat it with a little oil. Pour ½ cup of prepared batter into the hot pan and spread evenly. Cover with a lid and cook for 2 minutes. Flip the cake with a flat spoon.

Pour 1 tablespoon of tempering, and spread evenly. Cover and cook again until golden. Remove from pan, cut into wedges and serve with green chutney or sweet-sour pickle.

Note: You can use shredded cabbage, boiled corn or green peas, or chopped mixed boiled vegetables in place of bottle gourd.

Handva Atta

Grind together 1 cup skinless split green gram, 1 cup rice, ½ cup split Bengal gram and ¼ cup wheat to make a coarse flour.

Makes 3 cups

(Image on page 145)

Warm Pasta with Broccoli and Pesto

Serves 6-8

INGREDIENTS

For pesto

½ cup grated Parmesan cheese
1 cup basil leaves
1 cup spinach leaves
3-4 cloves garlic
¼ cup pine nuts
1 tsp salt
1 tsp pepper
¼ cup virgin olive oil

For pasta

250 gm pasta of your choice, (ziti, penne, rigatoni, fusilli or similar short pastas may be used; avoid long, noodle-like pasta).
500 gm broccoli, separated into florets
A pinch of soda bicarbonate
1 small red pepper, chopped
Salt to taste
Chilli flakes to taste

To garnish

Slivers of Parmesan cheese

METHOD

For pesto, place all the ingredients except olive oil in a food processor and blend until smooth. While motor is running pour olive oil in a thin stream and continue blending until all the oil is absorbed. Remove from blender and set aside in a bowl.

For pasta, boil the pasta for 7-8 minutes; make sure its *al dente* (cooked yet firm to the bite). Blanch broccoli in boiling water with a pinch of soda bicarbonate, drain and rinse with cold water and set aside.

To assemble, place warm pasta, broccoli and pepper in a large bowl. Toss with salt and chilli flakes. Spoon prepared pesto over the pasta and toss gently. Adjust seasoning. Garnish with Parmesan and serve warm or at room temperature.

Tawa no Handvo
Couscous
Ratatouille
Double Chocolate
Mousse Parfait

Christmas Punch
Shahi Paratha
Spiced Cottage Cheese Lukhnawi-Style
Creamy Salsa Tostadas

Spiced Cottage Cheese Lukhnawi-Style *Serves 6-8*

Lukhnawi Masala Paneer

INGREDIENTS

600 gm cottage cheese, cut into fingers
½ tsp turmeric powder
150 gm fried cashew nuts
1 medium onion, sautéed until browned
¼ cup ghee
½ tsp caraway seeds
150 gm onions, finely chopped
A pinch of turmeric
½ small onion, sliced
½ small pepper, sliced
½ tsp red chilli powder
½ tsp coriander powder
¼ tsp *garam masala*
¼ tsp pepper powder
½ cup thick tomato purée
1 small tomato, seeded and sliced
Salt to taste
¼ cup fresh cream

To garnish

Finely chopped coriander, slivered green chillies and ginger, and cream

To serve

Crisp *naan* or *roti*

METHOD

Soak cottage cheese fingers in a bowl of water with ½ teaspoon turmeric powder for 20 minutes. Make a paste of cashew nuts and sautéed onions and set aside. Heat ghee in a pan; add caraway seeds, and then add chopped onions, a pinch of turmeric. Sauté until brown.

Add sliced onions, pepper, cashew nut-onion paste, a little water, chilli powder, coriander powder, *garam masala* and pepper powder. Cook until fragrant. Add tomato purée, sliced tomato and salt. Cook gently. Add cottage cheese fingers and finish with cream.

Garnish with chopped coriander, green chillies, ginger and cream. Serve hot with *naan* or *roti*.

(Image on adjacent page)

Shahi Paratha

Serves 4

INGREDIENTS

For dough

250 gm sieved refined flour
¼ cup fresh cream
1-2 tbsp warm ghee
½ tsp caraway seeds
Salt to taste

For filling

150 gm skinless split Bengal gram
250 gm crumbled cottage cheese
2 tsp garlic paste
2 tsp ginger-chilli paste
2 tsp chilli powder
1 tsp pepper
1 tsp *garam masala*
1 tsp lemon juice
2 tbsp finely chopped coriander leaves
2 tbsp chopped cashew nuts
Salt to taste
Oil for frying

METHOD

For dough, make soft dough with flour, cream, ghee, caraway seeds and salt. Add little milk if the dough feels dry. Cover and set aside for 1 hour.

For filling, cook the split gram in enough water until soft. Allow it to cool. Add the remaining ingredients except oil in a bowl and mix well.

For *paratha*, divide the dough into 8 parts. Roll out each one to 5-6-inch circle. Apply little oil on the edge of rolled dough. Place 2-3 tablespoons filling on one piece and cover with the other rolled round. Press lightly and set aside until you finish with the rest of the dough.

Apply little oil on a hot frying pan and cook *paratha* on both sides, using little oil while flipping on other side. Press gently with flat spoon; cook until golden in colour. Serve hot with *raita*, vegetable or curry.

(Image on page 146)

Ratatouille

Serves 6

INGREDIENTS

5 tbsp olive oil
2 medium onions, sliced
4 cloves garlic, thinly sliced
3 medium brinjals, sliced
Salt to taste
Pepper to taste
3 medium zucchini, sliced
1 red pepper, sliced
1 green pepper, sliced
1 kg tomatoes, blanched and chopped
1 tsp fresh thyme
1 tsp oregano
2 bay leaves

To garnish

Chopped parsley

To serve

Prepared couscous

METHOD

In a heavy-bottomed frying pan, heat 2 tbsp of olive oil and sauté onions and garlic until soft. Remove from the pan and set aside. To the same pan, add 1 tbsp oil and fry the brinjals until soft, remove from pan, add salt and pepper and set aside. In the same pan, add the remaining oil and fry the zucchini.

When it is half cooked, add peppers and cook until soft. Now add the cooked brinjals, onion and garlic. Mix well. Stir in the tomatoes along with salt, herbs and bay leaves. Cook for 8-10 minutes.

Garnish with parsley. Serve, hot or cold with couscous, or as a vegetable accompaniment.

Note: This mixture also can be used as a filling for crêpes.

(Image on page 145)

Hyderabadi Biryani

Serves 8-10

INGREDIENTS

For rice layer

2 cups Basmati rice

1½ tsp salt

1 tbsp ghee

3 cloves

3 cinnamon sticks

3 cardamoms

1 bay leaf

1 tsp caraway seeds

For dal layer

1 cup split pigeon peas, washed and soaked

Salt to taste

3 green chillies

3 cloves

3 cardamoms

3 cinnamon sticks

¼ tsp turmeric powder

2 tbsp ghee

3 medium onions, sliced

1 bunch coriander leaves

½ bunch mint leaves

½ cup beaten yogurt

For masala paste

1 tbsp chopped ginger

1 tbsp garlic

12 dried red chillies, soaked in water

2 tbsp coriander seeds

2 tsp fennel seeds

2 tsp poppy seeds

½ cup freshly grated coconut

3 tsp chopped cashew nuts

To garnish

Fried cashew nuts, chopped coriander leaves

To serve

Beaten yogurt

METHOD

For rice layer, wash and soak the rice in 3½ cups water for 20 minutes. Bring water to a boil. Add rice, salt, ghee, cloves, cinnamon, cardamoms, bay leaf and caraway seeds. Cook until water is absorbed. Remove from heat and transfer rice to a dish and cool.

For *dal* layer, wash and soak the pigeon peas for 20 minutes. Boil just enough water with salt, green chillies, cloves, cardamoms, cinnamon stick, and turmeric powder.

Add the pigeon peas and cook until tender. Set aside. Grind together all the ingredients of the *masala* paste. Set aside. In another pan, heat ghee and fry the onions till golden brown. Reserve half for garnishing and to the remaining onions add the *masala* paste and fry until fragrant.

Add cooked pigeon peas along with coriander leaves, mint leaves and yogurt. Cook until the liquid is absorbed into the *dal*.

To assemble, preheat the oven to 150°C/300°F/Gas Mark 2. Take a flat-bottomed pan or a glass baking casserole and grease with ghee. Divide rice into 3 portions and *dal* into 2 portions.

Arrange the layers in the prepared pan or dish, beginning and ending with rice. Bake in the preheated oven for 15-20 minutes. Remove from the oven and garnish with reserved fried onions, cashew nuts and chopped coriander leaves. Serve hot with beaten yogurt.

Achari Aloo-Paneer ki Tahiri

Rice with Pickled Potato and Cottage Cheese

Serves 6-8

INGREDIENTS

3 tbsp ghee
1 inch cinnamon
5-6 cloves
5-6 cardamoms
2-3 bay leaves
½ tsp caraway seeds (*shahi jeera*)
2 medium onions, sliced
1½ cups long grain rice, washed and soaked in water
Salt to taste
10-15 baby potatoes, parboiled and halved
2 tbsp mixed pickle
250 gm cottage cheese, cubed and sautéed

To garnish

Sesame seeds and finely chopped fresh coriander, potato wafers

To serve

Yogurt

METHOD

Place a thick-bottomed pan on medium heat and add ghee. Add cinnamon, cloves, cardamoms, bay leaves and caraway seeds. Fry for a minute. Add onions and sauté for 2-3 minutes. Add soaked rice, salt and 3 cups water.

In a small bowl, toss potatoes and pickle. Add to the rice and continue cooking for 20 minutes or until potatoes and rice are soft. Add cottage cheese and mix. Transfer to a serving dish and garnish with sesame seeds, chopped coriander and arrange the wafers along the rim. Serve hot with yogurt.

Curried Lentil Pulao

Serves 8

INGREDIENTS

For rice

1½ cups long grain rice, washed and soaked

½ cup skinless split orange lentils, washed and soaked overnight

3 tbsp ghee

Salt to taste

For masala

3 tbsp grated coconut

5 cloves garlic

2 tsp coriander seeds

1 tsp cumin seeds

4 cardamoms

1 inch ginger

6 dried red chillies

½ tsp turmeric powder

For curry sauce

3 medium tomatoes, chopped

4 tbsp ghee

1 tsp sugar

Salt to taste

2 pinches of saffron threads

¼ tsp milk

For curry paste

2 medium onions

1 tbsp cashew nuts

1 tbsp almonds

1 tbsp coriander seeds

1 tbsp poppy seeds

2 tbsp aniseed

2 tbsp grated fresh coconut

1 inch ginger

2 green chillies

4 dried red chillies

3 cardamoms

3 cloves

3 cinnamon sticks

6-7 curry leaves

To garnish

Finely chopped coriander leaves

METHOD

Grind together all the ingredients of the *masala*. Set aside. For rice, cook rice and lentils separately in salt water. Drain and set aside. Make sure the grains are separate.

In a wide pan, heat ghee and fry the *masala* for 3-4 minutes. Add the rice, lentils and salt. Mix well and cook for 2 minutes. Remove from heat and set aside.

For curry sauce, cook the tomatoes with 1½ cups water, purée and sieve. Set aside. Grind together all the ingredients of the curry paste. Set aside.

In a thick-bottomed pan, heat ghee and add the curry paste; fry for 4-5 minutes. Add puréed tomatoes, sugar and salt. Mix saffron with milk and add to the sauce. Heat gently for 3-4 minutes.

To assemble, take a large piece of foil, place it in a glass casserole. Place rice in a pile in the centre and make a hollow at the top of the pile. Ladle half of the curry gently into the hollow. Pack the parcel tightly and place under the grill to heat it through. Remove from oven, open the foil, garnish with coriander leaves and serve hot with remaining curry at the side.

Subz Parda Pulao

Serves 8

INGREDIENTS

For dough cover

200 gm refined flour

¼ cup ghee

For pulao

⅓ cup ghee

200 gm sliced onions

3 tbsp ginger-garlic paste

3 tsp cinnamon-cardamom-clove powder

½ tsp sugar

300 gm chopped mixed vegetables (French beans, peas, cauliflower)

½ cup yogurt

½ cup milk

Salt to taste

250 gm Basmati rice

A pinch of saffron

To garnish

Fried onions, edible silver foil

To serve

Yogurt *raita*

METHOD

Preheat the oven 200°C/400°F/Gas Mark 6. For the dough, mix together both the ingredients for the dough with water and knead to make a soft dough.

For *pulao*, heat the ghee in a pan; add sliced onions and cook. Add ginger-garlic paste and cinnamon-cardamom-clove powder. Add sugar and roast the spices to bring out the colour. Add the vegetables, yogurt and sufficient water and cook until vegetables are *al dente* (cooked yet firm to the bite). Once vegetables are cooked, adjust the consistency of the gravy with milk, add seasoning and set aside.

Cook the rice separately and set aside. Mix saffron with little water and set aside. In a pan, put cooked vegetable mixture, cover with rice, add saffron water. Roll out the prepared dough and seal the pan.

Brush with little milk. Bake in preheated oven until the dough is brown in colour and properly cooked. Remove and cut open the dough from the centre. Garnish with fried onions and edible silver foil and serve hot with *raita*.

Subz Makhani

Serves 4

INGREDIENTS

1½ cups mixed boiled vegetables (carrots, peas, potatoes, cauliflower, French beans etc.)

Salt to taste

½ cup milk mixed with ½ tsp corn flour

For gravy

¾ cup water

3 cups chopped tomato

¼ cup chopped red pumpkin

½ cup chopped onions

2-3 cloves garlic, chopped

1 inch ginger, chopped

2 cloves

1 inch cinnamon stick

For tempering

1 tbsp ghee

½ tsp cumin seeds

½ tsp dried fenugreek leaves (*kasuri methi*)

1 tsp chilli powder

½ tsp turmeric powder

1 tsp *garam masala*

To garnish

Finely chopped coriander leaves and butter or cream

METHOD

For gravy, place a large pan on heat, add and mix all the ingredients for the gravy and cook till the vegetables are soft. Remove from heat, set aside to cool. Discard cloves and cinnamon. Drain out excess water. Blend the vegetables to a smooth purée and set aside.

For tempering, heat ghee in a pan; add cumin seeds, when they splutter, add dried fenugreek seeds, chilli powder, turmeric powder, *garam masala*. Roast for a few seconds and add boiled vegetables and salt. Cook for 2-3 minutes.

Add puréed vegetables and milk-corn flour mixture. Bring to a boil and then simmer until gravy is thick. Remove from heat and transfer to serving dish, garnish with coriander leaves and butter. Serve hot with *paratha*.

Pasta with Artichokes and Tomato Alfredo Sauce

Serves 4-6

INGREDIENTS

250 gm pasta, cooked
and tossed with olive oil

For sauce

1 cup milk

2 tbsp refined flour

1 tin (350 gm) artichoke hearts

1 tbsp butter

1 medium onion, finely chopped

1 cup chopped mushrooms

2 large tomatoes, blanched
and chopped

3-4 tbsp freshly chopped basil

Salt to taste

Pepper to taste

To serve

Parmesan cheese

METHOD

For sauce, mix together milk and flour in a pan and boil until thickened. Set aside. In a large pan place chopped artichokes with water and cook on low heat. In another pan melt butter and cook onion and mushrooms until slightly soft.

Add the tomatoes and basil. Add the mixture to the artichokes along with thickened milk. Season the sauce with salt and pepper. Mix well. Just before serving, heat the sauce and toss in the pasta. Sprinkle with Parmesan cheese. Serve hot.

Crêpes Stuffed with Orange and Almond Paste

Makes approx. 24

INGREDIENTS

For crêpes

100 gm whole-wheat flour

½ tsp salt or 1 tbsp sugar + a pinch of salt

1 tsp baking powder

1 cup milk

4 tbsp melted butter + for greasing

For filling

⅔ cup sweetened condensed milk

¼ cup orange juice concentrate

½ cup peeled and chopped fresh orange

2 tbsp toasted and ground almonds

½ cup whipped cream

For chocolate sauce

50 gm semi-sweet chocolate, chopped

1 tbsp butter

½ cup sweetened condensed milk

To garnish

Slivered almonds

METHOD

For crêpes, sieve together the flour, sugar or salt and baking powder. Mix this with milk to make the batter. Add melted butter and mix. Set aside. Place a thick-bottomed frying pan with 3-inch diameter circles over moderate heat and grease them with butter.

Pour 1 tablespoon of the batter into the circles and swirl the pan around so that the mixture spreads evenly over the base of the circles. Allow them to cook for 3-4 minutes and turn them over gently with a spatula and cook on the other side.

The pan shouldn't be too hot when you pour the batter. Continue until all the mixture is used up. Place the prepared crêpes on a large plate greased with butter and cover them with butter paper, until ready to use.

For filling, in a medium bowl, combine sweetened condensed milk and orange juice concentrate; mix well. Stir in orange and almonds. Fold in whipped cream. Keep in the refrigerator till ready to use.

For chocolate sauce, melt chocolate and butter over low heat in a small pan; stir in sweetened condensed milk. Cook, stirring constantly until mixture thickens slightly. Remove from heat and set aside. Makes ⅔ cup.

To assemble, take 1 warm pancake and place it on work surface; spoon 1 tablespoon filling and roll in jelly roll fashion or shape crêpe like a cone and fill with orange-almond filling. Drizzle with chocolate sauce and serve.

Chocolate Mousse Torte

Serves 8

INGREDIENTS

For base

50 gm cooking chocolate

2 tbsp cocoa powder

50 gm butter

175 gm digestive biscuits, crushed

2 tbsp powdered sugar

For mousse

1 tsp instant coffee powder

150 gm dark cooking chocolate

¼ cup fresh cream

1 tsp vanilla essence

½ cup whipping cream

3 tbsp powdered sugar

To decorate

Chocolate curls and whipping cream

METHOD

For base, lightly grease a 9-inch square/round loose-bottomed tin and line it with butter paper or foil. In a small bowl, place chocolate, cocoa powder and butter. Heat in the microwave for 1 minute or place the bowl over a pan of simmering water until melted. Stir until smooth.

Place digestive biscuits and sugar in a grinder to get fine crumbs. Stir into the melted chocolate mixture; transfer the mixture to the lined tin and, using the back of a spoon, press crumbs firmly in an even layer over the base and at the sides 1½-inch up the sides to form a casing. Chill while you make the filling.

For mousse, dissolve coffee in 4 tablespoons boiling water. Put the coffee, chocolate and fresh cream in a large bowl, rest it over pan of hot water until melted or in microwave for 1 minute. Stir until smooth. Add vanilla essence and set aside to cool.

Whip the cream with sugar until soft peaks form and gently fold into the cooled chocolate mixture. Pour this onto the biscuit crumb case and cover with foil or cling wrap. Chill for 2 to 4 hours or even overnight. Remove from tin and place on a serving plate; decorate with whipped cream and chocolate curls.

Choco-Berry and Chocolate-Mocha Shot Glass Desserts

Serves 12

INGREDIENTS

For choco-berry shot

1 cup milk

3 tbsp custard powder

3 tbsp fresh cream

4 tbsp sugar

½ tsp vanilla essence

1 cup whipping cream

6 tbsp chocolate chips

½ cup + 3 tbsp raspberry jam

1 cup crushed chocolate cookies (like Oreo)

3 tbsp icing sugar

To garnish

Fresh fruit

For chocolate-mocha

1 cup milk

3 tbsp custard powder

3½ tsp instant coffee powder

5 tbsp sugar

3 tbsp fresh cream

1 cup whipping cream

6 tbsp chocolate chips

3 tbsp icing sugar

1 cup crushed chocolate cookies (like Oreo)

½ cup Nutella (chocolate and hazelnut paste)

To garnish

Toasted and chopped hazelnut or coffee beans

METHOD

For choco-berry shot, heat the milk in a pan; in another bowl mix custard powder, fresh cream and sugar. Add the mixture to the boiling milk stirring continuously until thick. Place over a bowl of ice and cool completely. Add vanilla essence and mix. Whip the cream to form soft peaks. Add ½ cup whipped cream to the cooled custard. Fold in the chocolate chips. In the remaining whipped cream, add 3 tablespoons raspberry jam and mix well. Take a shot glass and layer in the following order: 1 tablespoon cookie crumbs at the base, 1 tablespoon custard, 1 tablespoon raspberry jam, 1 tablespoon cookie crumbs, and 1 dollop raspberry-flavoured whipped cream on top. Garnish with fruit and chill in a refrigerator before serving.

For chocolate-mocha shot, heat the milk in a pan; in another bowl mix custard powder, 2 teaspoons instant coffee powder, sugar and fresh cream. Add this to the boiling milk, stirring continuously until thick. Place over a bowl of ice and cool completely. Whip the cream to form soft peaks. Add ½ cup of whipped cream to cooled custard. Fold in the chocolate chips. In the remaining whipped cream, add 2 tablespoons icing sugar and 1½ teaspoons coffee powder and mix well.

Take a shot glass and layer in the following order: 1 tablespoon cookie crumbs at the base, 1 tablespoon coffee custard, 2 teaspoons Nutella, 1 tablespoon cookie crumbs, 1 dollop coffee-flavoured whipped cream. Top with chopped hazelnut or coffee bean. Chill in a refrigerator before serving.

Thandai Sorbet

Serves 6

INGREDIENTS

¼ cup Thandai Syrup (recipe follows)
½ cup milk
½ cup cold water

To garnish
Sliced pistachios and almonds
and rose petals

METHOD

Blend all the ingredients in a blender. Pour into aluminium tin and freeze for 6-8 hours or overnight. Remove and scoop out the frozen mixture and put through the blender. The mixture should be slushy. Pour it back into the tin and freeze again. When you want to serve, remove the tin and using ice cream scoop scrape the mixture and serve in small stemmed or shot glasses. Garnish with pistachios, almonds and rose petals.

Thandai Syrup

Heat 1 cup water and ½ cup sugar in a pan to make a thick syrup. Make a paste of 8 almonds, 8 pistachios, 2 tsp poppy seeds (soaked in water for 1 hour), 2 tsp aniseed, 2 tsp black peppercorn, 2 tsp melon seeds, 6-8 peeled cardamoms, and a pinch of saffron using 1 cup water. Sieve through a piece of muslin. Mix with the sugar syrup. Store in the refrigerator.

Makes 2 cups

Custard Apple Phirni

Serves 6

INGREDIENTS

4 tbsp long grain rice, soaked overnight

3 cups full fat milk

½-¾ cup sugar

1½ cups custard apple pulp

½ tsp powdered cardamom

To garnish

Sliced pistachios and a few threads of saffron

METHOD

Grind soaked rice to a smooth paste. Bring milk to a boil and add rice paste and sugar. Stir continuously until milk becomes thick and coats the back of the spoon and achieves custard like consistency. Remove from heat and allow it to cool completely.

Place in a refrigerator to chill. Once chilled, add custard apple and cardamom powder. Mix well and pour into earthen pot or a glass bowl. Chill for several hours. Garnish with pistachios and saffron. Serve cold.

Traditional Modak

Makes 10-12 modak

INGREDIENTS

2 tbsp oil

A pinch of salt

1 cup refined flour

For stuffing

¾ cup grated fresh coconut

½ cup crumbled jaggery

1 tsp roasted sesame seeds

½ tsp cardamom powder

½ tsp saffron

Ghee for moulding

METHOD

Heat 1 cup water in a thick-bottomed pan; bring to a boil. Add oil, salt and then the flour. Mix well until it forms smooth dough. Set aside for ½ an hour to cool.

For the stuffing, heat coconut and jaggery together till jaggery melts and forms a uniform mixture with coconut. Add the sesame seeds. Remove from heat and add cardamom powder and saffron. Mix well and set aside.

Divide the dough into small equal portions. Place one portion in the *modak* mould, from the base side, make hollow at the centre and stuff with coconut mixture and seal with additional dough. Repeat for remaining dough. Place all the *modak* on a sieve over boiling water and steam for 10-15 minutes. Serve warm after offering it to Lord Ganeshji.

Creamy Pistachio Fudge

Makes 24 squares

INGREDIENTS

Salad oil for greasing

400 gm white chocolate, cut into ½-inch pieces

¼ cup fresh cream

200 gm cream cheese, softened

1 cup icing sugar

½ tsp vanilla essence

½ tsp green food colouring

½ cup chopped pistachios

To garnish

Slivered pistachios

METHOD

Line 8-inch square tin with foil, allowing foil to extend to the sides of the tin. Grease with salad oil lightly. Melt chocolate and cream in double boiler until just melted or in a microwave for 1 minute. Set aside to cool. Beat cream cheese in a medium bowl and add icing sugar gradually.

Add the cooled chocolate mixture, vanilla and green colour. Beat well to mix. Stir in pistachios. Spread evenly in the prepared tin. Garnish with pistachios and chill in the refrigerator for at least 1 hour. Remove from pan by lifting the foil from the tin. Transfer onto a chopping board and cut into 1½-inch squares.

Chocolate Lava Cake

Serves 8

INGREDIENTS

150 gm refined flour
4 tbsp cocoa powder
1 tsp baking powder
1 tsp soda bicarbonate
150 gm butter + for greasing
100 gm caster sugar
150 gm thick yogurt
1 tsp vanilla essence
8 square pieces of dark chocolate
1-2 tbsp icing sugar

To serve

Vanilla ice cream

METHOD

Preheat the oven at 180°C/350°F/Gas Mark 4. Sieve the flour with cocoa, baking powder and soda bicarbonate. Set aside. Beat butter and sugar until light. Add the yogurt and beat well. Fold in the flour mixture alternating with 2-3 tablespoons water.

Add the vanilla essence and mix well. Grease 8 small aluminium or porcelain cups with butter and pour prepared batter till half full. Place 1 square piece of chocolate on top and push it inside slightly and smoothen the surface. Place on the middle rack of the oven and bake for 10-11 minutes.

Remove and invert on a serving plate, sprinkle with icing sugar. When you cut the cake from the centre, melted chocolate should ooze out. Serve immediately with vanilla ice cream.

Pistachio Naan Khatai

Makes 12

INGREDIENTS

½ cup powdered sugar

½ cup unsalted butter, softened at room temperature

¼ tsp nutmeg powder

¼ tsp cardamom powder

¾ cup refined flour

¼ tsp baking powder

A pinch of salt

¼ cup powdered pistachios

To garnish

Peeled and halved almonds

METHOD

Preheat oven to 150°C/300°F/Gas Mark 2. In a mixing bowl, combine powdered sugar, little at a time, with the softened butter until mixture is light and creamy. Add nutmeg powder and cardamom powder and mix well. Set aside.

In a separate bowl, sift refined flour with baking powder and salt. Add powdered pistachios. Combine flour mixture little at a time with butter mixture to form a soft dough. Wrap dough in plastic wrap and let it rest for 15-20 minutes. Knead the dough once again and divide into 12 equal portions.

Roll each portion into a smooth ball with no cracks. Press halved almond on each cookie and place on a cookie sheet lined with wax/parchment paper or lightly greased foil. Leave ample space between the dough balls.

Bake on the middle rack for 22-25 minutes (keep a close eye *naan khatai* should not brown). Remove from oven and let the *naan khatai* cool for 5 minutes before transferring to a cooling rack to cool completely before eating. Store in an air tight container at room temperature.

Double Chocolate Mousse Parfait

Serves 6-8

INGREDIENTS

12-14 Oreo cookies, cream removed and powdered

2-3 tbsp slivered almonds

For chocolate mixture

200 gm dark cooking chocolate

½ cup powdered sugar

½ cup fresh cream

1 tsp vanilla essence

1½ tbsp rum (optional)

1 cup whipping cream

For white layer

100 gm cream cheese, softened

100 gm condensed milk

1 tsp vanilla essence

1 cup whipping cream

¼ cup icing sugar

To garnish

Chocolate shavings and whipped cream

METHOD

Mix Oreo cookie crumbs with almonds; divide in half and set aside.

For chocolate mixture, combine chocolate with sugar and fresh cream and melt over boiling water. Stir until completely melted. Set aside to cool. Add vanilla essence and rum (if using). Beat the whipping cream over ice until stiff. Fold into the chocolate mixture. Set aside.

For white layer, beat cream cheese with condensed milk and vanilla essence in a small bowl until fluffy. Beat the cream with icing sugar in another bowl over ice until stiff. Fold into the cheese mixture. Set aside.

To assemble, take 6-8 transparent stemmed glasses. Sprinkle 1 part of Oreo crumbs at the bottom of each one. Spread chocolate mixture over it; smoothen the top. Sprinkle other part of Oreo crumbs and top it with cream-cheese mixture (white layer). Chill in the refrigerator for 1 hour. Garnish with chocolate shavings and whipped cream and serve.

(Image on page 145)

Multi-Cuisine

Corn and Water Chestnut Balls

Makes 20 balls

INGREDIENTS

400 gm fresh corn kernels, coarsely chopped
1 cup chopped water chestnut
1 cup spring onion
1 cup pepper
½ cup chopped mushrooms
¼ cup chopped basil and coriander
1½ tbsp powdered peanuts
1½ tbsp corn flour
2-3 finely chopped fresh red chillies
Salt to taste
Corn flour for rolling
Oil for shallow-frying

To serve

Sweet and Sour Sauce (recipe follows)

METHOD

Mix all the ingredients except the corn flour and oil in a bowl and mix well. Form 1-2-inch balls, roll each one in corn flour and shallow-fry in hot oil until golden. Serve hot with sweet and sour sauce.

Sweet and Sour Sauce

Mix together ½ cup unsweetened pineapple juice, ¼ cup cider vinegar, ¼ cup brown sugar, 1 tablespoon corn flour, 1 tablespoon finely chopped chillies, 2 tablespoons light soy sauce in a small pan; mix well. Place on heat and bring to a boil, stirring continuously. Remove from heat and set aside to cool.

Makes ¾ cup

Cheung Fun

Serves 6

INGREDIENTS

For batter

150 gm rice flour

1½ tbsp tapioca flour

2 tbsp corn flour

1 tbsp oil

½ tsp salt

For filling

1 tbsp finely chopped spring onions

200 gm tofu, cut into small cubes

For sweet sauce

1 tbsp vegetable oil

2 tbsp Hoisin sauce

1 tbsp brown sugar

1 tsp soy sauce

1 tsp sesame oil

To garnish

Finely chopped spring onion greens, sesame seeds and fried onion flakes

METHOD

Mix the rice flour, tapioca flour and corn flour together. Add 1½ cups water slowly and stir continuously. Add the oil and salt and mix thoroughly. Set mixture aside for at least an hour.

For the filling, mix together the spring onions and tofu and set aside. For sweet sauce, heat the oil on a small pan on low heat. Add the Hoisin sauce, brown sugar, soy sauce and sesame oil and stir continuously for about 3 minutes and remove from heat. Keep warm.

Prepare your steamer. Place an oiled plate on the steam tray. When the water is boiling, ladle and spread a thin layer of batter onto the preheated, oiled plate and sprinkle 1 teaspoon spring onion-tofu mixture.

Steam for about 3-5 minutes until the rice sheet is formed. Remove the plate from the steamer and using a flat spatula roll up the rice sheet and transfer to a plate. Drizzle with warm sweet sauce, garnish with spring onion greens, sesame seeds and fried onion flakes.

Isaan

Serves 6

Warm Vegetable and Tofu with Rice Balls

INGREDIENTS

½ cup grated carrot
½ cup chopped onion
½ cup chopped baby corn
½ cup chopped mushroom
½ cup and cubed and fried tofu
1 tbsp soy sauce
2 tbsp soy granules, soaked
½ tbsp roasted rice powder
½ tsp chilli paste
½ tsp garlic paste
1 tsp lemon juice
½ tsp sugar

To garnish

Finely chopped coriander leaves, chopped spring onion, chopped lime leaves and lemon grass

To serve

Sticky Rice Balls (recipe follows)

METHOD

Boil ½ litre water in a pan, add the vegetables and tofu. Cook until nearly dry and remove from heat and toss in remaining ingredients. Transfer the mixture to a serving plate and garnish with coriander, spring onions, lime leaves and lemon grass. Keep warm. Serve with sticky rice ball.

Sticky Rice Balls

To make sticky rice balls, soak the rice overnight in plenty of water. Steam the rice in bamboo basket or rice steamer. Take 1-2 tablespoons of rice and make walnut-sized balls. Use as required.

Pita Quesadillas with Cilantro Hummus

Serves 8

INGREDIENTS

For quesadillas

4 (7-inch) round pita breads, split crosswise

2 medium roasted red peppers, sliced

15-18 small spinach leaves, washed and trimmed

For coriander hummus

½ cup chopped coriander leaves

2 cloves garlic

1½ cups cooked chickpeas

2 tbsp lemon juice

2 tbsp tahina

2 tbsp olive oil

To serve

Spicy tahina sauce

METHOD

Preheat oven to 180°C/350°F/Gas Mark 4.

For coriander hummus, process coriander and garlic in food processor until chopped. Add chickpeas, lemon juice, tahina, oil, and ¼ cup water; purée for 3 minutes, or until creamy.

For quesadillas, place 4 pita halves on baking sheet. Spread each with ¼ cup hummus. Top with pepper, spinach, and remaining pita halves. Bake for 10 minutes, or until crisp. Cut into triangles, and serve with spicy tahina sauce.

Sun-dried Tomato Boursin Canapés

Serves 6

INGREDIENTS

100 gm Boursin cheese (garlic and herb flavoured)

5-6 sun-dried tomatoes, soaked in hot water

¼ cup thick yogurt or sour cream

1-2 tbsp olive oil

Salt to taste

Pepper to taste

12-14 small toasts or tart cases

To garnish

Finely chopped parsley and pine nuts

METHOD

Soften the Boursin in a bowl and set aside. Blend together soaked sun-dried tomatoes, yogurt, olive oil, salt and pepper in a blender until smooth. Fold in this mixture into soften boursin until mixed well. Cover the bowl with cling wrap and chill for an hour.

To serve, fill the mixture in a piping bag with star nozzle and pipe small stars on each toast. Garnish with parsley and pine nuts and serve.

(Image on page 179)

Open-faced Vegetable Taco with Salsa and Sour Cream

Makes 12-14 tacos

INGREDIENTS

12-14 (3-4 inch round) flat taco shells

1 cup refried beans

1 cup sautéed vegetables (zucchini, pepper, onions)

1 cup grated cheese

1 cup Red Salsa (page 71)

To garnish

Shredded lettuce and sliced jalapeño chillies

To serve

Sour Cream (page 71) and red salsa

METHOD

Make taco shell slightly crisp in the oven. Warm the beans and sautéed vegetables. In an oven tray, arrange taco shells ½-inch apart. Sprinkle grated cheese evenly on each one.

Place the tray under the grill until the cheese has melted. Remove from oven and spread 1 tablespoon refried beans on each taco shell, top it with sautéed vegetables and salsa. Garnish with shredded lettuce and sliced jalapeños. Serve at once with sour cream and salsa.

Herbed Bread Dip Mix

Makes 1 cup

INGREDIENTS

2 tbsp crushed chilli flakes
2 tbsp black pepper
2 tbsp dried oregano
2 tbsp rosemary
2 tbsp basil
2 tbsp parsley
2 tbsp garlic powder
1 tbsp salt
1-2 cloves minced garlic (optional)
1 cup virgin olive oil

METHOD

In a small blender jar, mix together all the ingredients except oil. Blend until well mixed. Remove and store in a jar. Place 1 tablespoon of this mix in a small deep bowl and pour olive oil till the bowl is half filled. Serve with bread of your choice as a starter.

Asian Clear Soup

Serves 8

INGREDIENTS

For stock

8 cups water
1 carrot
1 onion
5-6 black peppercorn
1 inch ginger or galangal
1 spring onion stalk
1 celery stalk
2 lemon grass stalks
1 bunch bok choy
2-3 Chinese cabbage leaves

To garnish

2 cups shredded cabbage leaves
2 cups bean sprouts
2 cups sliced fresh mushrooms
2 cups finely chopped spring onions
200 gm tofu, cut into small cubes
200 gm rice noodles, soaked in hot water
1 cup roasted and coarsely ground peanuts
2-3 tbsp coarsely ground dried red chillies
¼ cup soy sauce mixed with ¼ cup water
¼ cup rice vinegar
¼ cup chilli oil
¼ cup sugar water
¼ cup finely chopped coriander
4 tbsp chopped garlic, soaked in little vinegar and salt
500 gm fried wonton chips

METHOD

For stock, heat the ingredients of the stock in a large pan, and simmer for 30 minutes, sieve and transfer clear stock to ceramic or metal dish, and place on a burner at the table. Bring it to a boil.

Arrange all the garnishes in individual bowls and place them on the table. Diners cook their own portion of the vegetables, bean curd and season them to their own taste with garnishes and sauces. Each one should place some noodles in their bowls and top it with simmering stock to which they have added sauces. This soup is eaten as a final course.

Note: This is a popular dish in Asian countries is prepared for reunion family dinner, where everyone sits around a table and assembles their portion of soup in simmering broth.

(Image on page 180)

Mohinga

Serves 4-6

Dish of Noodles, Vegetables, Curry and Accompaniments

Mohinga is considered to be the national dish of Burma. It consists of noodles, vegetables and curry sauce with various accompaniments and sauces.

INGREDIENTS

250 gm noodles

1 tbsp sesame oil

500 gm mixed vegetables of your choice (broccoli, baby corn, peppers, zucchini, asparagus, mushrooms, carrots)

Salt to taste

For hot curry sauce

1 star anise

1 tbsp ground cumin seeds

1 tbsp turmeric powder

2-3 tbsp red Thai curry paste

1 large onion, finely chopped

2 cups coconut milk

¼ cup water mixed with 1 tsp corn flour

2-3 Kaffir lime leaves

A handful finely chopped coriander leaves

1 tbsp lemon juice

Salt to taste

For garnish and accompaniments

½-¾ cup finely chopped spring onion

½-¾ cup slivered fried garlic

½-¾ cup cubes of fried tofu

½-¾ cup toasted and ground peanuts

½-¾ cup sliced red or green chillies

½-¾ cup fried noodles

METHOD

Cook noodles as per instruction on the packet. Drain and set aside. Heat sesame oil in a wok; lightly stir-fry the vegetables for 1-2 minutes. Add salt and set aside.

For curry, dry-roast star anise in a small frying pan; add cumin powder and roast for 1-2 minutes. Add turmeric powder and Thai curry paste; cook for 3-4 minutes. Add onion and cook until soft. Sprinkle little water if required. Add coconut milk and corn flour mixture. Simmer for 10-15 minutes. Add lime leaves and coriander leaves. Finish with lemon juice and salt. Keep warm.

To garnish and serve, pile up noodles in a large plate, arrange the vegetables decoratively on top of them creating a big pile. Spoon some warm curry sauce over and top with fried noodles. Arrange the garnish ingredients around this in small bowls and additional curry sauce in a large bowl at the side.

Note: Provide soup bowls for each person to assemble their own noodles.

Falafel Salad

Serve 4-6

INGREDIENTS

8 Falafels (recipe follows)

4 cups mixed lettuce leaves, torn into 2-inch squares

2 medium tomatoes, seeded and cut into cubes

2-3 stems spring onions, thinly sliced

2 medium cucumber, thinly sliced and halved

½ cup sliced olives

¼ cup crumbled feta cheese

3 mint leaves, roughly chopped

1 tsp sumac

For dressing

½ cup thick yogurt

2 tbsp tahina paste

2 tbsp olive oil

1 tbsp lemon juice

¼ cup ice cold water

½ tsp salt

½ tsp pepper

To garnish

Paprika, as required

METHOD

For the dressing, mix all the ingredients in a small blender with ¼ cup cold water and process until smooth. Set aside in the refrigerator. Prepare all the vegetables as per the instructions given. Starting with lettuce leaves, pile up all the vegetables in a bowl.

Mix feta cheese, mint leaves and sumac in a small bowl and sprinkle over the vegetables. Cover with cling wrap and refrigerate until serving. Just before serving, place the falafel on the top; drizzle the dressing and toss the salad in down to up movement. Garnish with paprika and serve.

Falafel

Makes 24

INGREDIENTS

¼ kg split green gram

3 tbsp chopped coriander

3 green chillies, chopped

2 cloves garlic, crushed (optional)

9 onions, finely chopped

Salt to taste

1 tsp zatar spice mix

Oil for deep-frying

METHOD

Soak the gram in water overnight. Grind it in a grinder along with chopped coriander, chillies, garlic (if using) to a thick paste. Add salt. Just before frying the rissoles add onion and zatar.

Mix well. Take two spoons of the mixture onto your hand, flatten it with your finger and deep-fry 8-10 at a time on a medium heat in hot oil. Serve hot.

Watermelon and Feta Cheese Salad

Serve 8

INGREDIENTS

1 small onion, peeled, thinly sliced and halved

Juice of 2 lemons

1 kg watermelon, cut into 3-inch triangles and chilled

400 gm feta cheese, cut into ½-inch cubes

1 small bunch flat parsley, plucked into sprigs

1 bunch mint leaves, plucked, chopped and washed

3-4 tbsp virgin olive oil

½ cup sliced black olives

Freshly ground black pepper

Salt to taste

METHOD

Put sliced onions in a small bowl to steep with the lime juice, to bring out the transparent pinkness in the onions. Put watermelon and feta into large, wide shallow bowl. Add parsley and mint.

Tip the onions along with the juice over the salad in the bowl, add the olive oil and olives, then toss the salad very gently so that the feta and melon don't lose their shape. Add freshly ground pepper and salt. Check and adjust the seasoning before serving.

(Image on page 179)

Warm Lentil and Rice Salad

Serve 6

INGREDIENTS

1 cup whole red lentils, washed and soaked
1 cup long grain rice, washed and soaked
4 large onions, thinly sliced
4 cloves garlic, crushed
½ cup olive oil
¼ cup butter
2 tsp ground cinnamon
2 tsp paprika
2 tsp ground cumin-coriander
Salt to taste
Pepper to taste
3 spring onions, finely chopped

METHOD

Cook lentils and rice separately until grains are just tender; drain and set aside. Cook onions and garlic in oil and butter until very soft. Stir in cinnamon, paprika and cumin-coriander powder.

Cook for 2-3 minutes. Remove from heat and add drained rice and lentils. Transfer to a serving bowl and sprinkle with salt, pepper and spring onions. Mix well to combine. Serve warm.

Moroccan Eggplant Salad

Serves 6

INGREDIENTS

2 medium brinjals (eggplant), cut into 1-inch cubes
2 medium peppers, cut into 1-inch cubes
3 tbsp olive oil
1 medium onion, finely chopped
2-3 cloves garlic, minced
3-4 medium tomatoes, finely chopped
3 tbsp tomato purée
1 tsp chopped parsley
1 tsp paprika
½ tsp pepper
½ tsp turmeric powder
½ tsp cumin powder
Salt to taste

METHOD

Toss brinjal and pepper with 1 tablespoon olive oil and place under a hot grill until slightly charred. Remove the skin from vegetable and place in a bowl. In a heavy-bottomed pan heat remaining oil and fry onion and garlic until soft. Add the tomatoes, cook for 2 minutes and add tomato purée, parsley and all the spices. Cook for 1-2 minutes. Remove from heat and add brinjal and pepper. Toss well. Serve at room temperature.

Tomato Mould

Serve 6-8

INGREDIENTS

2 tbsp olive oil
2 onions, finely chopped
2 cloves garlic, finely chopped
2 cups tomato juice
1 bay leaf
Salt to taste
Pepper to taste
2 tsp gelatine soaked in
2 tbsp Vegetable Stock (page 23)
1 tsp lemon juice
2 tbsp cream cheese
100 gm fresh cream
1 tsp sugar
Dash of Tabasco

To garnish

Small bunches of parsley

To serve

Whole-wheat toast

METHOD

Heat the oil. Cook the onion and garlic. Add tomato juice, bay leaf, salt and pepper. Cook for 5 minutes. Slowly pour the gelatine mixture to the boiling tomato juice, stirring constantly. Add lemon juice and let it cool to room temperature.

Remove the bay leaf and blend the mixture in a processor. Add cream cheese, fresh cream, sugar and Tabasco and mix well. Pour this into a 1½ pint oiled mould and freeze it for 3 hours or overnight in a refrigerator. Unmould on a serving plate, garnish with small bunches of parsley and serve with crisp whole-wheat toast.

Injeera

Ethiopian Pancakes

Makes 20 pancakes

INGREDIENTS

1 tsp dried yeast
4 cups refined flour
1 tsp baking powder
Oil for cooking

To serve

Berbere (see recipe below)

METHOD

Dissolve yeast in 2½ cups water and add it to the flour. Mix well to make a smooth batter. Rest the mixture at room temperature overnight. Stir in the baking powder and set aside for 10 minutes.

Pour about ½ teaspoon oil in large skillet; add about ½ cup of the batter, and cook over low heat for 1 or 2 minutes. When bubbles appear, cover the skillet for 15 seconds. Remove from the skillet and place the pancake in a dish.

Repeat with the remaining batter, frying on one side only. The injeera are served at room temperature with vegetable dishes or spread with berbere (Ethiopian spice paste), rolled like a Swiss roll and served as a starter.

Berbere

Ethiopian Spice Paste

Makes 1 cup

INGREDIENTS

2 tsp cumin seeds
4 cloves
4 cardamoms
1 tsp coriander seeds
1 tsp fenugreek seeds
10 dried red chillies
½ tsp black peppercorns
1 tsp salt
½ tsp grated ginger
½ tsp cinnamon powder
¼ tsp turmeric powder
2½ tbsp paprika

METHOD

In a small frying pan, roast cumin seeds, cloves, cardamom, coriander seeds, fenugreek seeds and red chillies for 2-3 minutes. Remove from fire and allow it to cool. Add remaining ingredients and grind to a powder in an electric grinder. Store in an air-tight jar. Use with olive oil as required.

Makai-Masala Bhaat
with Kokum Saar
Sun-dried Tomato
Boursin Canapés
Arrabbiata Pizza
Watermelon and Feta
Cheese Salad

Asian Clear Soup

Water Chestnut and Batata Harrah Roll

Serve 4

INGREDIENTS

250 gm baby potatoes, half boiled and peeled

Oil for frying

3-4 tbsp olive oil

3-4 fresh red chillies, finely chopped

3 cloves garlic, crushed

250 gm water chestnuts, peeled and halved

Salt to taste

1 cup fresh coriander, finely chopped

For roll

4 medium-sized pita bread (thin variety)

½ cup tahina sauce (1 tbsp tahina mixed with ½ cup yogurt)

To serve

Chilli sauce, Garlic Mayonnaise (page 202) and slivered onions

METHOD

Fry the potatoes in hot oil until crispy and cooked. Drain on a paper towel. Heat olive oil in a large pan. Add chillies and garlic, cook for a minute or two. Add the potatoes, water chestnuts, salt and chopped coriander and cook gently, stirring until it wilts slightly. Remove from heat and set aside.

For roll, slightly warm the bread. Spread tahina sauce all over. Place ¼ of batata mixture in the centre; drizzle chilli sauce and garlic mayonnaise as per the taste, sprinkle with onions and roll in a jelly roll fashion. Wrap one end with paper napkin and serve with additional chilli sauce.

Crunchy Roasted Herbed Potatoes

Serve 4

INGREDIENTS

¼ cup olive oil

250 gm potatoes, cut into large cubes

2 tbsp freshly chopped herb (rosemary or parsley)

Sea salt to taste

Freshly ground pepper to taste

METHOD

Heat olive oil in a glass-baking dish for 2 minutes. Add the potatoes and toss to coat. Bake until cooked and crisp. Remove from oven and add the herbs, salt and pepper while still hot. Put it back in the oven for 2-3 minutes. Remove, transfer to a serving dish and serve.

Lebanese-style Green Beans

Serves 4-6

INGREDIENTS

2 tbsp olive oil

1 tbsp minced garlic

½ cup diced onions

¼ tsp cinnamon powder

450 gm green beans, cut into 1-inch pieces and blanched

½ cup Vegetable Stock (page 23)

2 tbsp chopped mint leaves

½ tsp salt

½ tsp pepper

1½ cups blanched and diced tomatoes

2 tbsp lemon juice

METHOD

Heat olive oil in a thick-bottomed frying pan. Add garlic, onions and cinnamon. Cook until soft. Add the beans, stock, mint leaves, salt and pepper. Bring to a boil and add the tomatoes and lemon juice. Cook until the juice becomes thick. Serve, hot or cold, as an accompaniment to Lebanese meal.

Turkish Roasted Potatoes

Serve 6

INGREDIENTS

4 large baking potatoes, washed
Salt to taste
Pepper to taste
10-12 black olives, halved

For topping

1 tbsp butter
2 medium onions, sliced
2-3 cloves garlic, crushed
Salt to taste
Pepper to taste
1 tbsp chopped parsley
1 tbsp oregano
1 tbsp chilli flakes
1 cup chopped tomatoes
½ cup grated Cheddar cheese
½ cup feta cheese

To garnish

Chopped chives or spring onion

METHOD

Preheat the oven to 150°C/300°F/Gas Mark 2. Prick the potatoes with a fork and wrap them in foil and bake for 30-40 minutes or until soft. Remove from oven, unwrap the foil and cut into large cubes, with the skin.

Toss with salt and pepper. Transfer to a greased baking dish, sprinkle the olives over and set aside. In a frying pan, melt butter and sauté onion and garlic until translucent. Add salt, pepper, chopped parsley, oregano, chilli flakes and the tomatoes.

Pour this over the potatoes and top it with both the cheeses. Bake in the oven until cheese melts and the potatoes are heated through. Garnish with chives or spring onion and serve hot.

Bameh Bil Zayt

Ladies' Fingers in Olive Oil

Serve 4

INGREDIENTS

500 gm fresh ladies' fingers, cut into ¼-inch pieces

¼-½ cup olive oil

1 cup finely chopped onion

3-4 cloves garlic, sliced

½ tbsp coriander powder

250 gm tomatoes, blanched and chopped

Salt to taste

A dash of sugar

A dash of all-spice powder

1 small fresh red or green chilli, chopped (optional)

To garnish

2-3 tbsp freshly chopped coriander

To serve

Prepared couscous

METHOD

Fry ladies' fingers in oil; drain and set aside. In the oil remaining in the pan, fry onion till transparent. Add garlic and coriander powder. Fry for 2 minutes. Add the tomatoes and cook further for 2 minutes.

Add fried ladies' fingers, salt, sugar, all-spice, chilli (if using) and ½ cup water. Cook gently over medium heat and bring to a boil.

Remove from heat and sprinkle chopped coriander. Serve as an accompaniment to a Lebanese meal or serve on the bed of couscous.

Teriyaki Tofu

Serves 6

INGREDIENTS

400 gm silken tofu, soaked in ice cold water

1 tsp salt

1 tsp pepper

2-3 cloves garlic, crushed

2 tbsp oil

Teriyaki sauce

6 tbsp cooking sake or rice vinegar

6 tbsp soy sauce

1 tbsp sesame oil

3-4 shallots, finely chopped

2 tbsp corn flour

2 tbsp raw brown sugar

To garnish

Finely chopped basil and toasted black and white sesame seeds

To serve

Wasabi Potatoes (recipe follows) and Sesame Spinach (recipe follows)

METHOD

Cut the tofu into 2-inch cubes. Drain tofu on a piccc of muslin or paper towel. Brush each cube with salt, pepper and crushed garlic. Set aside. In a small pan, mix together sake or rice vinegar, soy sauce, sesame oil, shallots, corn flour and sugar. Bring to a boil until sugar is dissolved and the sauce is little glossy. Set aside.

Heat 2 tablespoons oil in a frying pan; cook tofu cubes on both sides until slightly golden. Pile up tofu pieces on a serving plate, drizzle warmed teriyaki sauce over to coat tofu pieces. Garnish with basil and sesame seeds. Serve wasabi potatoes and sautéed spinach at the side.

Wasabi Potatoes

450 gm boiled and mashed potatoes, mixed with ¼ cup milk, 2 tbsp butter, 1 tsp wasabi paste, salt and pepper to taste.

Makes 2 cups

Sesame Spinach

Wash, drain and finely chop 2 cups spinach. Sauté in 1 tbsp butter and 2-3 cloves garlic. Add 1 tbsp sesame seeds and salt to taste.

Singapore-style Mee Goreng

Serves 4

INGREDIENTS

200 gm rice sticks or thick noodles

4 tbsp sesame oil

2-3 red chillies, slit

2-3 green chillies, slit

1 medium tomatoes, cut into wedges

4 spring onions, cut lengthways

200 gm broccoli, separated into florets

1 cup carrots, snow peas and French beans, cut lengthways

1 cup bean sprouts, washed

2 tbsp light soy sauce

Salt to taste

Paste

1 cup grated onion

4 cloves garlic

6-8 dried red chillies

1 tsp salt

1 tbsp sugar

2 tbsp chopped galangal

1 tbsp tomato sauce

To garnish

Fried tofu cubes, strips of red chilli and fried shallots

To serve

Peanut sauce and red chilli sambal

METHOD

Bring large pan of water to a boil and cook the noodles for 3 minutes. Drain and set aside. Grind the ingredients for the paste and set aside. Heat oil in a wok and fry the paste, chillies, tomatoes and spring onions till slightly wilted. Add broccoli, carrots, snow peas, French beans and bean sprouts.

Cook for 1 minute. Sprinkle a little water if you find the mixture too dry. Add the noodles, soy sauce and salt. Mix well. Transfer the noodles onto a serving dish and garnish with fried tofu, strips of red chilli and shallots. Serve hot with peanut sauce and sambal.

Hor Mok Phak

Steamed Coconut and Vegetable Custard

Serves 4

INGREDIENTS

1 tbsp corn flour

10 tbsp coconut milk

1 tsp +1 tbsp soy sauce

1½ tsp sugar

1 cup finely chopped mixed vegetables (Chinese cabbage, bok choy, cauliflower, carrot, baby corn, mushroom)

1 tbsp finely chopped Thai ginger

1 tbsp oil

1 tbsp red Thai curry paste

Coriander leaves for flavouring

Basil leaves for flavouring

2 banana leaves, cut into 5-inch oval shape and stapled together like a bowl

To garnish

Basil leaves, red chillies and coriander leaves

METHOD

Mix the corn flour with 2 tablespoons of water and set aside. In a small pan, mix together 4 tablespoons coconut milk, 1 tablespoon corn flour mixture, 1 teaspoon soy sauce and 1 teaspoon sugar. Heat gently to make a smooth paste and set aside.

Mix together vegetables and ginger. Heat oil in another pan; add red Thai curry paste and fry briefly. Add 3 tablespoons coconut milk and cook gently. When the mixture is fragrant, add the vegetables, remaining coconut milk, remaining soy sauce, remaining sugar. Mix well.

Cook for 3-4 minutes, stirring continuously. Add remaining corn flour mixture. Add coriander leaves and basil leaves for flavouring. Adjust coconut milk, if the mixture is too thick. Line the banana leaf cup with basil leaves.

Pour the vegetable mixture and top it with coconut milk-corn flour paste. Garnish with red chilli and coriander leaves. Place in a steamer and steam for 10 minutes. Serve hot with steamed rice.

Stir-Fried Vegetables with Ginger and Cashew Nuts

Serves 4-6

INGREDIENTS

2 tbsp oil

1 tbsp crushed garlic

1 tbsp red chillies

1 tbsp green chillies

¼ cup grated carrot

¼ cup chopped onion

¼ cup chopped tomato

¼ cup cubed and sautéed tofu

1 cup chopped mixed vegetables (cabbage, broccoli, mushroom, baby corn)

1 tbsp soy sauce

1 tbsp rice vinegar

Salt to taste

1 tbsp sugar water

¼ cup grated fresh ginger

¼ cup and toasted and chopped cashew nuts

To garnish

Sprigs of coriander and small red chillies

To serve

Rice or noodles

METHOD

Heat the oil in a wok; stir-fry garlic, red and green chillies, carrot, onion and tomato. Cook for 2-3 minutes. Add tofu, mixed vegetables and 6 tablespoons water. Cook for another 2-3 minutes.

Add soy sauce, vinegar, salt and sugar water. Mix gently and cook further for 2 minutes. Add ginger and cashew nuts and remove from heat. Garnish with coriander and red chillies. Serve hot with noodles or rice.

Barberry Rice

Serves 6-8

INGREDIENTS

2 cups long-grain Basmati rice

2 medium onions, thinly sliced

2 cloves garlic, peeled and crushed

⅓ cup olive oil

½ cup dried barberries (*zereshk*) washed, and drained

1 tbsp cinnamon powder

1 tbsp roasted cumin seeds

4 tbsp sugar

½ cup boiled chickpeas

½ cup halved cherry tomatoes

1 tsp powdered saffron dissolved in 4 tbsp hot water

2 tbsp plain yogurt

To garnish

Slivered almonds and pistachios

METHOD

Boil the rice in 4 cups water until all the water is absorbed. Remove from heat and set aside. In another pan, sauté the onion and garlic in 2 tablespoons olive oil, add barberries, cinnamon and cumin seeds; sauté for 1 minute over low heat because barberries burn very easily. Add 4 tablespoons sugar, mix well. Add cooked rice, mix well. Transfer to a bowl and set aside.

In the same pan, heat 4 tablespoons oil and 2 tablespoons water. Add chickpeas and cherry tomatoes; cook briefly and add prepared berry rice along with all the remaining ingredients. Toss well.

Grease an oven proof dish with little oil and transfer rice and even out the top. Cover rice with foil and cook on a low heat for 20 minutes. Remove from heat and garnish with almond and pistachios and serve hot.

Eggplant Crisps and Sun-dried Tomato with Skordalia

Serves 6

INGREDIENTS

For brinjal (eggplant)

18 one-fourth-inch thick brinjal slices

2 cups milk

Salt to taste

Pepper to taste

1 cup tempura batter mix

½ cup breadcrumbs

Olive oil for deep-frying

¾ cup sliced fresh basil leaves

For sun-dried tomatoes

50 gm sun-dried tomatoes, soaked in hot water

¼ cup olive oil

1 large clove garlic, sliced

1 tsp dried thyme

For skordalia (Greek-style garlic dip)

1 head garlic

1 tbsp olive oil

400 gm potatoes, peeled and cubed

¼ cup fresh cream

¼ cup butter

1 tbsp sour cream

1 cup almonds, roasted and powdered

1 tbsp lemon juice

1 clove fresh garlic, minced

Salt to taste

Pepper to taste

To garnish

Black olives tossed in olive oil and sour cream

METHOD

For the brinjal, in a large bowl, soak brinjal slices in milk for 1 hour. Drain; pat dry. Sprinkle brinjal lightly with salt and pepper. Make tempura batter as per instruction on the packet. Dip brinjal slices in this batter and then roll them in breadcrumbs, coating completely; place on baking sheet. Heat olive oil in heavy-bottomed large frying pan over medium heat. Working in batches, add brinjal slices to the pan and deep-fry until golden, about 2 minutes per side. Using slotted spatula, drain on paper towels. Sprinkle with salt and pepper.

For sun-dried tomatoes, mix all ingredients in large bowl and set aside. This can be made 2 days ahead. Cover and refrigerate.

For the skordalia, preheat the oven to 180°C/350°F/Gas Mark 4. Cut the top ½ inch of garlic head, exposing the cloves. Place garlic in small ovenproof dish; drizzle with oil. Cover tightly with foil and bake until cloves are soft, about 50 minutes. Cool. Squeeze garlic head from bottom to release garlic from skins.

Cook potatoes in medium-sized pan of simmering salted water until tender when pierced with fork, about 12 minutes; drain. Set aside. Bring cream and butter to simmer in a large pan. Remove from heat; whisk in sour cream.

Add potatoes to cream mixture and mash. Mix roasted garlic, ground almonds, lemon juice, and minced fresh garlic into potatoes. Season with salt and pepper.

To assemble, place 1 tablespoon skordalia in centre of each of 6 plates. Top skordalia with 1 brinjal slice, 1 tablespoon skordalia, 1 tablespoon sliced basil leaves, 1 sun-dried tomato, 1 brinjal slice, 1 tablespoon skordalia, 1 tablespoon sliced basil leaves, 1 sun-dried tomato, and 1 more brinjal slice. Garnish with olives and sour cream and serve.

Thai Noodles with Fried Basil

Serves 4-6

INGREDIENTS

200 gm rice noodles (3mm or 5mm)

2 tbsp oil

2 tbsp fresh red chilli-garlic paste

2-3 hand full of mixed vegetables (bean sprout, cabbage, bok choy, mushrooms, carrots, broccoli)

3-4 spring onions, cut into 2-inch pieces

100 gm grated tofu, fried in little oil

1 tbsp black bean sauce

1 tbsp soy sauce

1 tsp raw brown sugar

To garnish

Handful of fried basil leaves and roasted and powdered peanuts

METHOD

Blanch rice noodles as per packet instruction. Set aside. In an iron wok, heat oil, add chilli-garlic paste, fry for 1 minute. Add the vegetables, cook on high heat for 3-4 minutes. Add all the remaining ingredients. Transfer to a serving plate, Garnish with fried basil and roasted peanut powder. Serve immediately.

Moussaka-style Pasta

Serves 8

INGREDIENTS

For pasta

200 gm packaged pasta of your choice

3 tbsp olive oil

6 cloves garlic, crushed

1 tbsp basil, chopped

Chilli flakes to taste

Salt to taste

Pepper to taste

For grilled vegetables

500 gm mixed vegetables of your choice (brinjals, onions, peppers, broccoli etc.)

2 tbsp olive oil

1 tbsp mixed herbs

Salt to taste

For spicy tomato sauce

2 tbsp olive oil

2 medium onions, finely chopped

2 cloves garlic, crushed

100 gm tomatoes, blanched and coarsely chopped

2 tbsp tomato purée

1 tsp sugar

2 tsp salt

2 tsp freshly ground pepper

1 tbsp chilli flakes

1 tsp dried oregano

For topping

100 gm feta cheese

¼ cup fresh cream

Salt to taste

Pepper to taste

Paprika to taste

To garnish

Grated Parmesan cheese and freshly chopped herbs

METHOD

Preheat the oven to 170°C/325°F/Gas Mark 3.

For the pasta, boil the pasta in salted water till *al dente* (cooked yet firm to the bite). Drain and place under running cold water. Drain. In a large frying pan heat olive oil, add garlic, basil and chilli flakes and fry it for two minutes on a medium heat. Add drained pasta, salt and pepper. Set aside.

For the grilled vegetables, cut all the vegetables into cubes and place them on a baking tray. Drizzle olive oil, toss gently until it coats the vegetables. Sprinkle herbs and salt and toss again. Place under a grill for 7-8 minutes. Remove and set aside.

For tomato sauce, in a pan, heat oil, add onions and garlic, cook over medium heat until soft. Add tomatoes, tomato purée, sugar, salt, pepper and chilli flakes. Reduce heat, cover and cook for 30 minutes, stirring occasionally. Press through a sieve into a bowl, adjust seasoning and add oregano. Set aside.

For the topping, blend all the ingredients together in a blender jar and set aside.

To assemble, grease a glass baking dish with little olive oil. Toss prepared pasta with grilled vegetables and place them on a baking dish. Cover the pasta with tomato sauce and smoothen the surface. Gently pour the feta cheese mixture covering the top. Sprinkle with Parmesan cheese and bake in the pre-heated oven for 15-20 minutes. Remove from oven, garnish with herbs and serve hot.

Risotto Primavera

Serves 6

Springtime Vegetable Rice

INGREDIENTS

5 tbsp butter

2 stems spring onion, finely chopped

2-3 cloves garlic, crushed with little salt

1½ cups mixed vegetables of your choice (asparagus, peas, carrots)

1½ cups risotto rice (Arborio or Carnaroli)

1 glass dry white wine (optional)

5 cups Vegetable Stock (page 23)

Salt to taste

Pepper to taste

½ cup grated Parmesan cheese

½ cup thick cream

To garnish

A handful of freshly chopped herbs

METHOD

Melt 2 tablespoons butter in a heavy-bottomed pan; add spring onion and garlic as soon as butter becomes frothy. Sauté them till translucent but not coloured. Add the vegetables and cook until soft.

Sprinkle rice and stir until translucent, but do not allow it to brown. Pour on white wine (if using) and continue stirring to prevent rice from sticking. Cook until completely reduced. Heat the stock separately, and add it gradually to the rice little by little stirring constantly, ensuring that the rice can absorb each addition.

Season with salt and pepper. Just before rice is cooked, stir in Parmesan cheese and the remaining butter with a fork. Cover and keep till the right consistency is reached. Rice should be tender but not too soft. Add the cream just before serving. Garnish with freshly chopped herbs.

Potato and Courgette Pie

Serves 8

INGREDIENTS

For potato pastry

½ cup refined flour

½ tsp salt

½ tsp pepper

½ tsp mustard

¼ cup butter

½ cup mashed potatoes, mixed with 1 tbsp butter

For filling

2-3 tbsp butter

3-4 medium courgette (zucchini), cut into ¼-inch slices

2-3 cloves garlic, crushed

1 tbsp parsley

1 cup mushrooms, washed and sliced

500 gm tomatoes, blanched and chopped

½ cup breadcrumbs

½ cup sour cream

1 tbsp chopped almonds

1 tsp paprika

1 tsp salt

½ cup Parmesan cheese

METHOD

For the potato pastry, sieve together the flour, salt, pepper and mustard powder. Rub butter into the flour with your fingertips. Add mashed potatoes and add a little cold water; knead to make a firm dough. Refrigerate for 5-7 minutes.

Roll the pastry and press it in 8-inch pie dish, prick with fork and bake it in hot oven at 180°C/350°F/Gas Mark 4 for 8-10 minutes or until golden. Remove from oven.

For the filling, melt 2 tablespoons butter in a frying pan, sauté courgette in batches, stirring occasionally for about 8-10 minutes. Melt remaining butter, fry garlic, parsley and mushroom until soft, for about 3 minutes.

Add the tomatoes and cook for 3 more minutes. Stir in breadcrumbs, sour cream, almonds, paprika and salt. Mix well. Remove from heat and add cooked courgettes. Spoon the mixture over prepared pie crust and sprinkle Parmesan on top.

Bake in a hot oven at 180°C/350°F/Gas Mark 4 till the top is golden. Remove from oven and let it rest for 5-7 minutes. Cut into wedges and serve.

Cottage Cheese and Green Pea Biryani

Serves 10-12

INGREDIENTS

For rice

2 tbsp ghee

3-4 cardamoms

3-4 cloves

3-4 cinnamon sticks

3-4 peppercorns

2-3 bay leaves

2 cups rice, washed and soaked in water

Salt to taste

A pinch of saffron mixed with ¼ cup milk

For green pea mixture

4 tbsp ghee

2 medium onions, sliced

6 cloves garlic, chopped

2-3 green chillies, chopped

½ inch ginger, crushed

2 tbsp *garam masala*

Salt to taste

250 gm cottage cheese, cut into small cubes

½ cup green peas, boiled

1 large tomato, finely chopped

To garnish

½ cup onions, sliced and golden fried

To serve

Spiced yogurt

METHOD

For the rice, heat ghee in a wide pan; add cardamoms, cloves, cinnamon sticks, peppercorn and bay leaves. Add soaked rice, salt and 3 cups water. Boil for 10-12 minutes till rice is almost done. Drain and reserve the water.

For the green pea mixture, heat ghee in a pan; add onions and fry until golden brown. Add garlic, green chillies, ginger and *garam masala*. Fry for 1 minute. Add ½ cup water and salt. Bring to a boil. Add cottage cheese, peas and tomato. Cook on a low heat. Remove from heat and set aside to cool.

To assemble, take a thick-bottomed pan or a round baking dish. Grease it with little ghee. Spread half of the rice and top it with peas mixture, smoothen the surface. Cover with remaining rice. Sprinkle ¼ cup reserved rice water.

Sprinkle saffron-flavoured milk over the rice. Sprinkle the rice with little melted ghee. Cover the dish with foil and bake in the hot oven at 180°C/350°F/Gas Mark 4 for 10-15 minutes. Remove the foil and garnish biryani with fried onions. Serve hot with spiced yogurt.

Grilled Vegetables and Tagliatelle with Almond Sauce

Serves 6

INGREDIENTS

For grilled vegetables

500 gm mixed vegetables of your choice (brinjals, onions, peppers, zucchini, broccoli etc.)

2 tbsp olive oil

1 tbsp mixed herbs

Salt to taste

For pasta

250 gm tagliatelle pasta

1 tbsp butter

1 tbsp freshly chopped parsley

50 gm slivered or grated Parmesan cheese

Salt to taste

Pepper to taste

For almond sauce

½ cup slivered almonds

2 tbsp butter

3 tbsp oil

2 tbsp refined flour

2 cups Vegetable Stock (page 23)

½ cup milk

Salt to taste

Pepper to taste

½ cup fresh cream

To garnish

Freshly chopped herbs, toasted and slivered almonds

To serve

Crisp bread and grated Parmesan cheese

METHOD

For the grilled vegetables, cut all the vegetables into 2-inch sticks and place them on a baking tray. Drizzle olive oil; toss gently until it coats the vegetables. Sprinkle herbs and salt, toss again. Place under a grill for 7-8 minutes. Remove and set aside.

For the pasta, boil the pasta as per instructions on the package. Drain and rinse. Melt butter in a pan; add parsley and cook for 30 seconds. Add pasta, Parmesan, salt and pepper. Toss gently and set aside.

For almond sauce, roast almonds in melted butter on low heat until slightly golden. Place in a blender jar and blend until smooth. In a medium pan, heat oil and add the flour. Cook slightly till golden brown.

Remove from heat and add vegetable stock. Bring to a boil, lower the heat and add powdered almonds, milk, salt, pepper and lastly the cream. Continue cooking, stirring continuously. Boil until thick. Remove from heat and set aside.

To assemble, at the time of serving, heat pasta on low heat and toss grilled vegetables until well mixed. Heat almond sauce separately and add to pasta mixture. Toss gently again. Transfer to a serving dish, garnish with fresh herbs and slivered almonds. Serve hot with crisp toast and Parmesan cheese.

Makai-Masala Bhaat with Kokum Saar

Serves 4-6

INGREDIENTS

4-5 tbsp ghee

¼ tsp asafoetida

1 tsp mustard seeds

A few curry leaves

2-3 green chillies, slit

2-3 cinnamon sticks

2-3 cloves

½ tsp turmeric powder

1 medium onion, sliced

½ cup corn kernels, boiled

10-12 ivy gourd, cut into 4 pieces vertically

1½ cups rice, washed, soaked in water for 10 minutes and drained

2 tsp *kala masala*

2 tsp *garam masala*

1 tsp chilli powder

Salt to taste

2 tbsp cashew nuts, chopped

2 tbsp grated fresh coconut

1 tsp lemon juice

1 tsp ginger juice

To garnish

¼ cup freshly chopped coriander leaves

To serve

Kokum saar and fried *pohe che papad*

METHOD

Heat ghee in a thick-bottomed pan; add asafoetida and mustard seeds. When they splutter, add green chillies, cinnamon, cloves and turmeric powder. Add onion, corn and ivy gourd. Cook for 2-3 minutes and add the rice and all the dry spices. Stir and add 3 cups of water. Cover and cook on a low heat for 15 minutes, stirring occasionally.

Add salt, cashew nuts, grated coconut, lemon juice and ginger juice. When rice is soft and cooked, remove from the heat and garnish with coriander leaves and serve with *kokum saar* and *pohe che papad*.

Note: You can also use cauliflower, French beans, brinjal etc instead of the vegetables used in the recipe.

(Image on page 179)

Pasta and Mushrooms with Pangrattato Topping

Serves 4

INGREDIENTS

For topping

1 cup coarse breadcrumbs made from baguette

2 tbsp olive oil

2-3 cloves finely chopped garlic

2 tbsp finely chopped flat parsley

2 pinches chilli flakes

Salt to taste

Pepper to taste

For pasta

2 tbsp butter

2 tbsp olive oil

1 medium onion, finely chopped

2 cloves garlic, crushed

500 gm fresh mushrooms, washed and quartered

1 tsp dried oregano

Salt to taste

Pepper to taste

1 cup Vegetable Stock (page 23)

½ cup toasted walnuts or pine nuts

¼ cup Parmesan cheese

¼ cup fresh cream

200 gm pasta of your choice

To garnish

Bunch of parsley

To serve

Crusty bread

METHOD

For the topping, spread out breadcrumbs in a shallow baking pan and bake, stirring time to time, until golden. Cool completely in the pan. Heat the oil in a thick-bottomed pan and fry garlic, parsley, chilli flakes, salt, pepper and breadcrumbs until crisp. Set aside in a jar.

For pasta, heat butter and olive oil together in a heavy-bottomed frying pan on moderate heat. Add onion, and garlic. Cook until soft. Add mushrooms, oregano, salt, pepper and vegetable stock. Cook until mushrooms are browned.

Stir in the nuts, Parmesan and cream. Meanwhile cook the pasta in salted boiling water, uncovered, until *al dente* (cooked yet firm to the bite). Drain and transfer to a baking dish. Pour the mushroom mixture over the pasta, sprinkle crumb topping and bake in a hot oven at 180°C/350°F/Gas Mark 4 for 15 minutes or until the top is golden. Garnish with parsley and serve with crusty bread.

Baked Broccoli Tortillas

Serves 6-8

INGREDIENTS

12 (7-inch) round flour tortillas made with milk

For filling

400 gm broccoli, separated into small florets

Salt to taste

1 tbsp vinegar

2 tbsp butter

1 medium onion, finely chopped

4-5 tbsp grated cheese

For sauce

500 gm tomatoes, blanched and coarsely chopped

200 gm grated Monterey Jack cheese mixed with 1 tbsp maize flour

2 tbsp oil

1 clove garlic, crushed with a little salt

1 bay leaf

1 tbsp finely chopped parsley

1 tbsp chives

1 tbsp oregano

Salt to taste

Pepper to taste

½ cup grated Monterey Jack cheese

METHOD

For the filling, boil salted water with vinegar and drop broccoli florets till tender or for about 7 minutes. Drain and set aside. Melt butter in a frying pan and cook onion until soft. Add the broccoli and sauté for 2-3 minutes. Remove from heat. Add 4-5 tbsp grated cheese and set aside.

For the sauce, mix together the tomatoes and Monterey jack cheese-maize flour mixture in a blender jar and blend until smooth. Heat oil in a pan; fry garlic for 1 minute. Add the tomato mixture, bay leaf, herbs, salt and pepper. Add a little water if the sauce is too thick.

To assemble, roll up broccoli mixture in the tortillas and arrange in an oven-proof serving dish. Pour the sauce over and sprinkle with ½ cup grated cheese. Bake in a hot oven for 10 minutes and serve hot.

Arrabbiata Pizza

Makes 4 eight-inch pizzas

INGREDIENTS

For dough

2 tsp dried yeast

½ tsp sugar

2½ cups refined flour

1 tsp salt

9 tbsp olive oil

2 cups Arrabbiata Sauce (recipe follows)

400 gm mozzarella cheese

METHOD

For the dough, preheat the oven to 230°C/450°F/Gas Mark 8. Sprinkle the yeast and sugar into ¼ cup lukewarm water. Let it stand for 2-3 minutes, then stir the yeast and sugar mixture until sugar is dissolved. Put it in a warm place for 5-7 minutes, or until the yeast bubbles up and doubles in volume.

Sift flour and salt in a large bowl. Make a well in the centre and pour the yeast mixture and 3 tablespoons oil. Mix the dough with your fingers. When you can gather it into a rough ball, place the dough on a floured board and knead till it is smooth and elastic. Dust lightly with flour, place it in a bowl, cover and keep it in a closed oven till double in size.

When you want to use the dough, remove and knead it again on a floured board. Divide the dough into 4 parts. Roll out one part into an 8-inch circle. Place it on a large baking sheet. With your thumbs, crimp the edge of the circle until it forms a little rim. Brush the surface with little oil. This prevents the dough from getting soggy.

Pour ½ cup of arrabbiata sauce and spread evenly with the back of a spoon. Sprinkle ½ cup mozzarella cheese and 1 tablespoon oil and bake it in the lowest shelf of oven until crust is lightly browned. Repeat this for the rest of the dough.

(Image on page 179)

Arrabbiata sauce

Makes 1½ cups

INGREDIENTS

1 tbsp olive oil

3-4 cloves garlic, crushed

1 medium onion, finely chopped

4-5 tomatoes, blanched and chopped

½ tsp salt

½ tsp pepper

1-2 tsp chilli flakes

1 tbsp finely chopped basil

1 tbsp finely chopped parsley

4-5 tbsp fresh cream

METHOD

For the arrabbiata sauce, heat oil in a pan; fry garlic and onion until soft. Add tomatoes, salt, pepper and chilli flakes. Bring it to a boil and add herbs. Remove from heat and set aside. Gently add the cream and mix well. Use as required.

Pizza Dough Variation:

Cornmeal dough: Substitute 1 cup refined flour for equal amount of maize flour.

Herbed dough: Add 3 tablespoons of freshly chopped herbs while kneading the dough.

Whole-wheat dough: Substitute 1 cup of refined flour for an equal amount of the whole-wheat flour.

Spicy dough: Add 2 tablespoons ground paprika and 1 tablespoon black pepper to the flour while sieving with salt.

Garnish Variation:

Alternatively, you can garnish the pizzas with strips of green, red or yellow peppers, or sliced olives, onions and capers, or sliced tomatoes and basil leaves, or sliced mushrooms or boiled yellow corn kernels.

Basic Recipes

Mayonnaise *Makes 1 cup*

Place 1 egg, ½ tsp salt, ½ tsp pepper, ½ tsp mustard powder and ½ tsp sugar in a blender jar and blend at medium speed. When thoroughly blended, add ½-¾ cup salad oil or olive oil in a very thin stream, blending at high speed. Do not add oil too quickly or the mayonnaise will curdle. After it has thickened, add 2 tbsp vinegar or lemon juice and continue blending until mixed completely. Taste and adjust the seasoning. Store in an airtight jar in the refrigerator.

Variation:

Aïoli or garlic mayonnaise: Add 2 cloves garlic while blending the mayonnaise.

Curry mayonnaise: Add 1 tsp curry powder and 2 tbsp finely chopped onion to mayonnaise.

Eggless Mayonnaise *Makes 1½ cups*

In a stainless steel bowl, combine 200 gm fresh cream with 2 tsp mustard powder, ½ tsp salt, ½ tsp pepper and 2 tbsp sugar. Place over a bowl of crushed ice and beat with a beater until thick. Gradually add ¼ cup salad oil or olive oil till completely absorbed into the cream. Stir in 3 tsp vinegar or lemon juice and chill until ready to use.

Vinaigrette Dressing *Makes ½ cup*

Mix together 3 tbsp cider vinegar, 1 clove garlic, minced, 1 tsp mustard, 1 tsp sugar, 1 tsp salt, ½ tsp pepper, ½ tsp Italian seasoning and ¼ cup olive oil in a screw top jar. Cover and shake vigorously for 10 seconds. Use as required. Store in the refrigerator.

Herbed Bread Croûtons *Makes 1 cup*

Preheat the oven to 220°C/425°F/Gas Mark 7. Melt ½ cup butter, add 2 tbsp mixed herbs (basil, sage, oregano, tarragon), mixture of 1 tsp garlic powder and 1 tbsp salt or ¼ tbsp garlic salt . Remove from heat and pour this in a baking tray. Toss 200 gm day old bread, cut into bite-sized cubes in this mixture till all the pieces are well coated. Bake in the hot oven for 5-10 minutes until golden brown.

Glossary

English	Hindi
Aniseed	Saunf
Apricot	Khubani
Asafoetida	Hing
Broad beans	Sem
Buttermilk	Chaas
Caraway seeds	Shah jeera
Cardamom	Elaichi
Carom seeds	Ajwain
Chickpeas	Kabuli chana
Chickpeas	Kabuli chana
Chillies, round, red	Boria mirch
Cinnamon	Dalchini
Coriander seeds	Dhania
Cottage cheese	Paneer
Cudpahnuts	Chironji
Cumin seeds	Jeera
Custard apple	Sitafal
Dates	Khajur
Dill	Suva
Fenugreek leaves, dried	Kasoori methi
Fenugreek seeds	Methi dana

English	Hindi
Green peas	Matar
Kidney beans	Rajma
Lemon grass	Chai ki patti
Maize flour	Makkai ka atta
Mushrooms	Khumb
Mustard grains, split	Rai ki dal
Nigella seeds (onion seeds)	Kalonji
Nutmeg	Jaiphal
Peanuts	Moongphali
Pine nuts	Chilgoza
Plain flour	Maida
Pomegranate	Anaar
Poppy seeds	Khuskhus
Rock sugar	Mishri
Saffron	Kesar
Semolina	Rawa/sooji
Spring onions (scallions)	Hara pyaaz
Walnuts	Akhrot
Water chestnut	Singhara

Glossary of Terms

Appetiser	A first course of a meal of tidbits, drinks or cocktails
Barbeque	To cook on a rack over a charcoal fire or gas
Beat	To work a mixture smooth with regular, hard, rhythmic movements
Blanch	To immerse briefly in boiling water
Boursin	Soft, creamy French cheese
Compote	Fruit or vegetables stewed or cooked in sugar syrup
Croquettes	A soft mixture of vegetables and seasoning, rolled into oval shapes coated with breadcrumbs or vermicelli and fried
Croûtons	Small pieces of bread, fried or toasted
Dry-roast	To heat/lightly fry without fat; usually spices, on a griddle (*tawa*)
Dust	To sprinkle lightly with flour or sugar
Feta	Greek cheese made from a mixture of sheep's and goat's milk
Fold in	To combine a light, whisked or creamed mixture with other ingredients so that it retains its lightness
Garnish	To decorate food
Gelatine	Unflavoured gelatine granules used to set a mixture
Grease	To coat the surface of a dish with fat to prevent sticking
Grenadine	Pomegranate syrup
Grill	To cook over or under dry heat; barbeque
Paprika	Spice made from dried bell peppers or pepper
Parfait	A light, cream enriched, iced dessert, often with fruit purée
Praline	Sugar flavoured with coarsely-ground roasted nuts
Sieve	To rub or press moist or dry food through a sieve
Stir-fry	To fry quickly over high heat in a lightly oiled pan (as in a wok), while stirring continuously
Sun-dried tomatoes	Tomatoes that are dried in the sun for a number of days and then stored or preserved in olive oil
Taco seasoning mix	A special blend of Mexican spice that is a combination of dried onion, garlic, chillies and other spices
Temper	To heat spices in oil before adding to a dish
Toss	Toss to mix ingredients in a quick, light way, till thoroughly blended